GIFTS & NATIONS

For Stanley Hoffman—
in appreciation of
many gifts of
insight.

Wilton
Dillon

Abby Aldrich Rockefeller Folk Art Museum,
Colonial Williamsburg Foundation, Williamsburg, VA

GIFTS&
NATIONS

With a new afterword by the author
WILTON S. DILLON

With a new preface by *Mary Catherine Bateson*
and a foreword by *Talcott Parsons*

Transaction Publishers
New Brunswick (U.S.A.) and London (U.K.)

Second printing 2004
New material this edition copyright © 2003 by Transaction Publishers, New Brunswick, New Jersey. Originally published in 1968 by Mouton.

This book is printed on acid-free paper that meets the American National Standard for Permanence of Paper for Printed Library Materials.

Library of Congress Catalog Number: 2003042628
ISBN: 0-7658-0545-6
Printed in the United States of America

Library of Congress Cataloging-in-Publication Data

Dillon, Wilton.
    Gifts and nations : the obligation to give, receive, and repay / Wilton S. Dillon ; with a new preface by Mary Catherine Bateson, a foreword by Talcott Parsons, and a new afterword by the author.
        p. cm.
    Originally published: The Hague ; Paris : Mouton [1968].
    Includes bibliographical references and index.
    ISBN 0-7658-0545-6 (pbk. : alk. paper)
    1. Economic assistance, American—France. 2. Economic assistance—Psychological aspects. 3. Gifts—Psychological aspects. 4. International relations—Psychological aspects. I. Title.

HC276.2.D55 2003
338.91'73044'09044—dc21   2003042628

To Alfred Kroeber, Margaret Mead, and Claude Lévi-Strauss
whose many gifts are traveling in my kula ring

CONTENTS

PREFACE TO THE TRANSACTION EDITION

Reading *Gifts and Nations* is very much like looking into what Barbara Tuchman called "a distant mirror." Wilton Dillon did the research on which this study is based in the 1950s. A great deal has changed since then, both in world affairs and in anthropology, yet this book resurfaces at a time when many of the issues it raised are once again coming into prominence. Dillon uses French reactions to the Marshall Plan to explore more general, and still highly important, issues related to international giving, material and intellectual, issues that are both particular and universal. Today, in a time of intensifying exchange and interaction between nations, with all the benefits and dangers that this involves, we are in urgent need of increased understanding of how such interactions result sometimes in friendship and sometimes in resentment and antagonism.

The Marshall Plan, through which the United States supported European recovery after World War II, was a shining landmark in the history of international relations. This study is particularly focused on the transfer of ideas about the organization of industry through technical assistance programs. Op eds and letters to the editor continue to call at regular intervals for "a new Marshall Plan," but even with the ending of the Cold War, most aid is given in direct relation to strategic goals. Because of the great disparities between developing and developed nations, the ambivalence about aid felt by both donor and receiver nations that Dillon describes continues, but today it is highlighted by a sharpened internal debate in many nations even about aid given to fellow citizens in need. The United States today is intensely concerned, in the aftermath of the Cold War, with propagating ideas and instructing the world on the benefits of capitalism, free trade, and democratic government. As the only remaining superpower, all of America's partnerships are out of balance, with the United States expecting to lead and teach. The United States lacks sensitivity to the responses of other nations as it claims roles associated with seniority, greater wisdom, or greater virtue – or in some cases past oppression.

We live today with a primary rhetoric of competing rights. This is a work that deals with obligations, offering a useful balance, especially since it deals with interlocking, reciprocal obligations. There are voices today that argue the *obligation to give*, but few that recognize that giving is but one of a triad, complemented by an *obligation to receive* and an *obligation to repay*. It is the fulfillment of this interlocking set of obligations that weaves the social fabric of reciprocity and interdependence, while receiving gifts without a means of material or symbolic reciprocation is potentially demeaning. Dillon explores the French perception that the Americans they dealt with half a century ago failed to acknowledge their intellectual contributions – a failing he himself gracefully addresses by analyzing the entire issue through the work of Marcel Mauss, a follower of Durkheim. This gives the book a very contemporary feel, for in the interval since the 1960s a whole range of French theorists have become important to American intellectuals. One thinks first of Mauss's own intellectual heir, Claude Levi-Strauss, but many others come to mind: Derrida, Foucault, Braudel, Bourdieu, Lacan, and so on.

Another factor that gives this book a contemporary feel is the renewed interest in qualitative methodologies, especially in intensive work with the narratives of individual informants, both in anthropology and in cultural studies. Dillon began his interest in gift exchange in Japan, where he served on the Civil Information and Education staff of General MacArthur during the Occupation. His reading of Ruth Benedict's *The Chrysanthemum and the Sword* inspired him to become an anthropologist as he found her hypotheses relevant to his work of interpreting Western civilization to the Japanese. When he left Berkeley for Columbia to study with Alfred Kroeber and Margaret Mead in 1951, Mead encouraged him to explore the relevance for France of some of Benedict's ideas about the Japanese concept of obligation. Building on techniques developed at the Columbia University Research in Contemporary Cultures, Dillon worked intensively with a French manufacturer. Dillon also met with his companions on delegations to the United States, watching and listening as the Frenchman's appreciation for what he was learning from the U.S. was accompanied by satisfaction at the anti-Americanism of de Gaulle and at expressions of French independence.

2

Interest in this tradition has just now been beginning to revive, but meanwhile anthropologists continue to be largely unavailable for thinking about international relations. It is to be hoped, as the United States gives – or offers – or demands the role of leader, that it will also discover the balancing obligations – to receive guidance, recognizing alternative points of view and the wisdom of other civilizations.

Mary Catherine Bateson

FOREWORD

It is a privilege to have the opportunity to write a brief foreword to Dr. Dillon's little book. There seem to me to be two main bases on which it merits careful attention on the part of a considerable range of people, both theoretically interested technical social scientists and people concerned with the policies of organizations, not only in the international field, but within countries as well.

The more obvious of these is the highly original and I think valuable contribution the author makes to the understanding of what to many have been puzzling as well as disturbing features of the development of American foreign policy and the reactions of other countries to it. Dr. Dillon gives what, to me, is by a good deal the most penetrating analysis with which I am familiar of the negative elements in the reaction of so many Frenchmen, and eventually of the French Government, especially through the action of General de Gaulle, to what most Americans, and many others, have considered to be the generosity of the aid program which crystallized with the Marshall Plan in 1947. Of course back of this has lain the military 'aid' which eventually, in 1944 and 45, rescued France from her humiliating status of German occupation. Again, as in 1917-18, it seems probable that, without American intervention, the position of France would have been considerably less happy than in fact it was.

Dr. Dillon's analysis, stressing as it does the importance of balancing the system of relations between the giving of gifts and the reciprocation by the beneficiaries of such gifts, is impressively illuminating. His thesis, which he well documents, that the main source of the trouble has lain in American incapacity to define ways in which the recipients could *repay* the gifts they had received, rings true and merits a great deal of thought in its bearing on future, indeed current policies.

One of the great merits of Dr. Dillon's thesis is that it is capable of

5

generalization from the original empirical reference. Hence I stressed above that it was probably applicable not only to international relations, but to relations within particular societies. Indeed this capacity for generalization derives from the fact that it is based on the work of an eminent theorist in the social field, the French anthropologist-sociologist Marcel Mauss. Even though Mauss' work, as that of perhaps the most important single continuer and improver of that of Émile Durkheim in France, was in one sense highly visible, especially in the between-the-wars period, he may nevertheless be to a degree compared with Gregor Mendel, a man who formulated some very basic principles, but in such an 'oversimplified' form that their highly generalized significance could not immediately be apprehended. Dillon has done more than simply to call attention to Mauss and his work, entering a plea to stop neglecting its importance. He has, by applying its principles in a field which Mauss himself did not consider, contributed greatly to the presumption of the high generality of the principles which Mauss set forth.

It is finally, significant that the Dillon study comes along at a time when a 'breeze' of theoretical concern with the importance of relations of 'exchange' and 'interchange' in social relations has begun to blow with considerable force. Within the French tradition itself, Claude Lévi-Strauss gave it the first main impetus after Mauss – to whom his debt is clear and fully acknowledged. In the United States, economics has been considered, theoretically, a very isolated discipline. However, certain aspects of its concern with exchange have begun to be generalized to a wider context, albeit with many qualifications. Among economists, perhaps Kenneth Boulding has gone farthest. Among sociologists, George Homans, Peter Blau and James Coleman have received a great deal of attention. The present author has also made a few attempts to work in this direction. Perhaps this is the beginning of a major new development in the sciences of human social behavior. I think Dr. Dillon has made a major contribution to this development.

Talcott Parsons
(Harvard University)

6

ACKNOWLEDGMENTS

I am pleased over the coincidence that the material in this study, written in 1960 first as a doctoral dissertation at Columbia University, should now appear in book form in the wake of the 20th anniversary of the speech at Harvard University during which General George C. Marshall launched the European recovery program bearing his name. Historical and primitive perspectives on the Marshall Plan are increasingly pertinent now that such a scheme has become the symbol of large-scale, international philanthropy as well as the kind of effort needed to increase the chances of the disadvantaged within a given society.

Another famous general deserves thanks for providing the public behavior which symbolizes the substance of this book: General Charles de Gaulle, for his reactions to 'gifts' from the United States. I am as indebted to his help in dramatizing my subject matter as to his countryman, Marcel Mauss, for the ideas with which I could analyze some of the sources of stress and strain within the Atlantic community.

Many of my intellectual debts in the preparation of this study are acknowledged in the introduction. I refer to those gifts in the form of ideas and facts which came from professors' lectures, books, conversations with friends and colleagues, and questions from students when, from time to time, I found myself in front of a classroom, a part of the process of giving, receiving, and being repaid.

As man does not live by ideals alone, I am indebted to the United States Government and several foundations for money that allowed me to travel and have the necessities of life during the pursuit of knowledge. In 1951-1952, I studied in Paris and Leyden on the G.I. Bill, and, at the same time, started the first phase of the field work represented in this study. The investigation in 1954 was partly financed by the Society for Applied Anthropology. The Society contributed to my travel expenses within Europe to visit social science research centers in preparation for my duties as Director of the Clearinghouse for Research in Human Organization. In 1956, the Grant Foundation made a grant to Overseas Training and Research, Inc., to enable my wife and me to return to France for three additional months of field work. For interviews in Paris in 1958 and 1959, I am indebted to the Ford Foundation for a study travel grant to Africa which permitted stops in Paris. A brief visit to Paris in 1960, adding to the final documentation of this study, was made possible by an African assignment from the Hazen Foundation and the Phelps-Stokes Fund. For time needed in 1960 for the final preparation of the manuscript, I owe a great deal to the understanding and cooperation of the trustees of the Hazen Foundation and the Phelps-Stokes Fund and their presidents, respectively, Dr. Paul J. Braisted and Dr. Frederick D. Patterson, who relieved me from research and administrative duties to complete this task before starting new field work in Ghana and Togo.

The late Professors Donald G. Tewksbury and Lyman Bryson of Columbia University Teachers College gave me unusual counsel and assistance during the early phases of this study. Prof. Tewksbury, with a deeper Asian background than my own, helped to re-orient me to the Western world. He made me aware of common elements in the historical processes at work in traditional societies in Asia and Europe. He also showed me, by his own example, the thrill of seeing wholly the branches of learning. Resisting but not disdaining specialization, he remained faithful to both the mandarin scholar ideal of versatility and the thought process we associate with the undifferentiated men of Renaissance Italy. Thus he found nothing alien in Marcel Mauss when I proposed the French sociologist as a source of concepts for analyzing my thesis material on international relations. Prof. Bryson gave me excellent preparation for studying anthropology in Europe. He saw contemporary developments in empirical social science in the United States from the perspective of philosophical and humanistic traditions in Europe and England.

For assistance in a variety of ways in France, I am indebted to: Monsieur and Madame B. and their children, who appear in this study; officers of the French Association for the Increase of Productivity (A.F.A.P.); Mlle Yvonne Oddon, librarian of the Musée de l'Homme, Paris; the late Monsieur Émile Pinson, who tried to teach me how to be a Frenchman; Monsieur and Madame François Pinson, who gave me shelter and comfort; Prof. François Bourricaud and Mlle Anne-Marie Goguel, who bought their knowledge of Max Weber and Talcott Parsons to bear on helping me to understand their own society; members of the Division of Social Sciences at UNESCO, who provided stimulating colleagueship; Dr. Jean-Roger Herrenschmidt, for hours of conversation and helpful criticism; Clemens

Heller, for hospitable introductions to scholars and working space at the École Pratique des Hautes Études; and Madame Robert Sartin, Countess Guymon de Roffignac and the Count and Countess de Sélancy, for hospitality and insights into the Alsace-Lorraine variants of French society, as well as common denominators of European cultures.

Dr. David S. Landes gave me encouragement and support for continuing research on the interplay between French family and business behavior, a subject on which he had done some pioneer work. His counsel in both Paris and New York brought me to greater hope for future collaboration between historians, economists, and anthropologists. In discussing my materials with Professors Jacques Barzun and Shephard Clough of Columbia, I also received historical perspectives on the intellectual background of industrialization in France.

Beyond the considerable legacy of thought, insight, and discipline provided by Dr. Margaret Mead, I am grateful for her insistance and expectation that I fulfill my obligation to scholarship despite my distractions by ephemeral current events in New York City and in the new capitals of Africa.

Dr. Rhoda Métraux helped me to see the possibilities of qualitative and comparative analysis of materials in this study. She also gave generously her time and suggestions in the organization of the manuscript. Miss Gladys Burkhart brought editorial wisdom to her typing the manuscript.

My wife served as a willing helpful informant when, as a result of my studies of gifts and obligations in France, I wanted to find out something about reciprocity and exchange in American culture. To Marcel Mauss' descriptions of the universals in gift exchange, she added her particular knowledge of how to handle obligations in a tradition and kinship-oriented county in rural Virginia, thereby helping me to realize my studies have just begun.

Finally, I Wish to thank Professors Conrad Arensberg, Ruth Bunzel, Solon T. Kimball, Mead, and Sloan Wayland for their Socratic probing and the models they provided of how to stretch curiosity without losing sight of evidence.

GIFTS & NATIONS

Everything is stuff to be given away and repaid

MARCEL MAUSS

CHAPTER I

INTRODUCTION

A. PURPOSES

This study has one objective and two related, subsidiary aims. The objective first is to seek a greater universality for the ideas of Marcel Mauss (1872-1950) related to gift exchange. His essay, *The Gift: Forms and Functions of Exchange in Archaic Societies*, is the source of ideas that will be examined in the context of organized technical assistance relationships between groups in two societies of Western industrial civilization, France and the United States.[1] The question is: Do generalizations about the social process of exchanging gifts among pre-literate and ancient men apply to people who live in modern, industrial societies?

Large-scale organization of technical assistance among nations was not known to Mauss at the time he analyzed archaic societies.[2] Foreign aid as a governmental activity of both big and small nations did not develop to great importance until the end of World War II. Mauss isolated three types of obligations which he found widely distributed in human societies in both time and space. These obligations will be the focus of our inquiry and will form the headings for the three main chapters: 1) the obligation to give; 2) the obligation to receive; and 3) the obligation to repay. They refer to the feeling and relationships simply expressed by the notion that if the person gives something to another person, both are likely to feel a strain

1. Originally published as 'Essai sur le don, forme et raison de l'échange dans les sociétés archaïques', in *L'Année Sociologique*, second series, 1923-24. It was republished in French in C. LÉVI-STRAUSS, ed., *Sociologie et Anthropologie* (Paris: Presses Universitaires de France, 1950), pp. 145-279. The English translation by Ian Cunnison, published in 1954 by the Free Press, Glencoe, Ill., will be quoted throughout this study.
2. In personal correspondence, October 19, 1959, Lévi-Strauss, the collector and interpreter of Mauss' complete works, *op. cit.*, wrote: 'I doubt very much that Mauss ever spoke or wrote about international technical assistance, since this was practically unknown at the time when his scientific activity was interrupted, about 1940.'

unless the receiver gives something back to the donor. Emphasis here will be given to the obligation felt by the receiver (the French) to make countergifts.

I shall regard as outside the scope of this study a critical treatment of how Mauss reached these generalizations after an examination of ethnographic data describing gift exchange institutions and practices (e.g., the Maori, Samoans, Andaman islanders, New Caledonians, Trobrianders, Northwest Coast Indians of North America, and the ancient Romans, Hebrews, Germans, and Hindus). It is sufficient for my purposes that an effort be made to discover whether his generalizations, which I assume to be valid vis-à-vis his data, are useful in understanding the giving and receiving process marking the relations between certain Americans and Frenchman during the years 1951-1960.

A subsidiary aim of the inquiry is to analyze the 'something' that is given. I want to find out if knowledge and intellectual goods are comparable to tangible gifts. Mauss wrote that 'Everything is stuff to be given away and repaid.' He made no explicit analyses of knowledge or techniques as gifts. Thus one aim will be to examine the cross-cultural learning process by which adults in one society receive, from adults in another society, gifts in the form of knowledge of machines and the techniques of organizing and managing work. I wish to show that the giving, receiving and repayment process involving knowledge as a commodity is not unlike the process of handling beads, pottery, food or other tangible objects which circulate among people and become a part of their networks of building up and discharging obligations.

Knowledge about productivity will be the 'something' to be analyzed as a gift. Americans offered, and Frenchmen received, knowledge of how more goods can be produced at lower prices through the ways men organize themselves and their machines. The transformation of the knowledge after it has been given and then handled by the receiver, and the possibility of its going back to the donor in a new form, is to be described in an empirical case study of gift exchange involving a French informant, Monsieur B. The flow of tangible and intellectual goods between donors and receivers is influenced, it will be demonstrated, by culturally determined differences in peoples' responses to the obligations to give, receive and repay.

The other subsidiary aim of this study is to describe the strains and the compensatory mechanisms which seem to operate when persons of donor-teacher' nations and persons of 'pupil-receiver' nations lack an institutionalized means of discharging obligations toward each other. In Chapter IV, 'The Obligation to Repay,' an analysis will be made of a sequence of personal and international events to provide suggested answers to the questions: What happens when human beings who feel indebted to others are

14

frustrated in their efforts to discharge their obligations? Why are they frustrated? What kind of substitutes do they find for their desire to return gifts?

The quest for reciprocity then is another way of phrasing the central subject matter of the study. People who give, desire something in return. People who receive, want to give something in return. Both are involved in the quest for reciprocity.

In reaching his generalizations, Mauss gave special attention to Malinowski's *Argonauts of the Western Pacific*, a classic study of how obligations are handled by Melanesians.[3] Going to Malinowski's original description of the *kula* ring, a complex institution of international ceremonial exchange, I have Mauss' interest justified. Mauss analyzed the Malinowski material comparatively with other ethnographic data. I have used it to provide a primitive perspective on the French quest for reciprocity in their relationships with American donors. Through an understanding of the *kula*, it is possible to see more clearly the aspects of human organization which contribute to a steady relationship between donors and receivers. A comparison between South Sea and North Atlantic exchanges suggests that harmonious, stable relationships are more likely to occur, and strain to be reduced, when a system is worked out by which everybody can be a potential donor. The roles of donor and receiver are reversed at intervals by participants of the *kula* ring. The absence of mechanisms for reversing the flow of goods or ideas from the receivers in the North Atlantic alliance to the donors (Americans) is a striking contrast. A *kula*-type exchange system, if invented for organized technical assistance among nations, would appear to have a better chance to perpetuate itself and give satisfaction to all the participants than does a system which has not yet invented techniques, awarences or institutions to allow recipients to get rid of obligations by returning gifts to which all attach value. Instead of the *kula* principle operating in the Marshall Plan, the aid effort unwittingly took on some of the characteristics of the potlatch ceremony of the 19th century among North Pacific Coast Indians in which property was destroyed in rivalry, and the poor humiliated. This is the general conclusion to be reached in this study.

The last chapter will discuss some of the implications of this case study. Taking a cue from Mauss, who also went beyond his data to speculate on the application of his knowledge to human affairs, I wish to suggest: a)

3. BRONISLAW MALINOWSKI, *Argonauts of the Western Pacific: An Account of Native Enterprise and Adventure in the Archipelagoes of Melanesian New Guinea* (New York: E. P. Dutton, 1953), xxxi + 527 pp. Originally published as Monograph No. 65 of the London School of Economics and Political Science and based on the Robert Mond Expedition to New Guinea, 1914-1918.

some proposals for future research; and b) some guide-lines for persons responsible for planning the negotiations, treaties or agreements leading to foreign aid programs.

In introducing the materials of this study, I shall proceed first with three other sections of background:

1. a detailed account of the natural history of the inquiry, including the materials ,and methods used and acknowledgements to other social scientists for previous research and advice which have been helpful here;

2. a brief interpretation of the place of Marcel Mauss in the recent history of French sociology and his contributions to this study; and

3. a schematic summary of the sequence of events encompassed by this inquiry so that the reader may have an overview of the empirical materials before reaching the interpretations and comparisons in the three main chapters.

B. MATERIALS AND METHODS USED IN THIS STUDY: A NATURAL HISTORY

In a recent essay, 'On Intellectual Craftsmanship,' C. Wright Mills states that 'method' has to do with how to ask and answer questions with some assurances that the answers are more or less durable, and that 'theory' has to do with paying close attention to the words one is using, especially their logical relations.[4] Furthermore, in calling for a method and theory that will bring clarity of conception, economy of procedure and 'the release rather than the restriction of the sociological imagination,' Mills reminds the working social scientist that:

To have mastered 'theory' and 'method' is to have become a self-conscious thinker, a man at work and aware of the assumptions and the implications of whatever he is about. To be mastered by 'method' or 'theory' is simply to be kept from working, from trying, that is, to find out something that is going on in the world. Without insight into the way it is done, the results of study are infirm; without a determination that study shall come to significant results, all method is meaningless pretense.[5]

This study makes no claim to be a model of theory or method. However, I have enjoyed the unusual advantages of being able to study one individual's attitudes and behavior at intervals over a period of nine years. Such a diachronic perspective[6] has allowed me to see both changes and

4. This essay appears in L. GROSS, ed., *Symposium on Sociological Theory* (Evanston and White Plains: Row, Peterson & Co., 1959), p. 25.
5. *Ibid.*
6. See MARGARET MEAD, 'Character Formation and Diachronic Theory' in MEYER FORTES, ed., *Social Structure* (Oxford: Clarendon Press, 1949).

regularities in thought and action. To the retrospective view of my informant of his own life, in the context of a long national history, I have been able to add my own knowledge of the informant's life based on observation and taking part in many of the events described in the nine-year period. Thus I have been able to find a social process at work. Its main outlines would not be so clear without the time dimension. Moreover, by concentrating on a network of interpersonal relations maintained by one man and embracing a variety of French institutions and several social ranks, I have been able to respond to the challenge of a tradition of social research calling for both *in vivo*[7] inclusiveness and specific sequences of behavior. The path to this point has not been smooth or direct. Rather, it has followed a route described by John Dollard in his *Criteria for the Life History*:

> Every scientific worker has felt the anxiety associated with an insecure grasp on his object of research. Many of us, too, know the feeling of fumbling while trying to find the right way to think about a given problem. Very often the worker will proceed for his whole scientific life with a gnawing sense, appearing perhaps only at intervals, that he has never gripped his material in a satisfying way.[8]

In outlining below the various stages through which this study has moved in its natural history,[9] I will trace the steps of such wondering and searching for a satisfying grip of the materials. The findings, gathered by interviews and direct observation, and then subjected to comparisons with behavior described in studies of other societies, have been sifted through a variety of conceptual frameworks from several disciplines. For example, 'cross-cultural learning' derives from both anthropology and psychology; 'interaction' and 'equilibrium' are concepts found in anthropology, sociology, and the biological sciences; 'autonomy' and 'self-esteem' are psychological concepts; an interest in childhood training and its relations to adult personality and the dynamics of institutions grows out of the work of anthropologists and psychiatrists. Moreover, my self-consciousness about the relationship between myself, as the interviewer, and the informant has been conditioned by studies of interview phenomena by clinical psychologists, psychiatrists, anthropologists, and students of public opinion. Communication and information theory has been studied by engineers, humanists, and anthropologists. All have contributed to my understanding of the

7. Cf. CONRAD M. ARENSBERG, 'The Community-Study Method' in *The American Journal of Sociology*, Vol. LX, No. 2 (Sept. 1954), p. 109.
8. New Haven, Conn.: Yale University Press, 1935, p. 1.
9. Cf. SOLON T. KIMBALL, 'The Method of Natural History and Educational Research,' in G. SPINDLER, ed., *Education and Anthropology* (Stanford: Stanford University Press, 1955), p. 82.

behavior of persons in different cultures who are involved in transactions of giving and receiving. Both directly and indirectly, these concepts have contributed to a 'release of the sociological imagination' and the eventual use of gift exchange as a framework for finding out something that is going on in the modern world, namely, what is the process by which complex human groups, called nations, organize their relationships to exchange knowledge and thereby practice mutual aid.

The final choice of Mauss' ideas on gifts and obligations as an organizing framework, however, does not mean that other abstractions are without value for gathering and interpreting the data of this study. The opposite is true. A choice had to be made for purposes of exposition. The data could be interpreted also by such conceptual schemes as represented by: communication, interaction, cross-cultural education, and acculturation. In fact, a synthesis could be made to suggest that these words can refer to the same observable phenomena. A Frenchman boarding an airplane to fly to the United States is an observable event one can analyze as a single element in a process which can be described by one or all of these conceptual tools.[10]

I prefer a theory of gifts and obligations because of inductive procedures which led me to see French styles of reciprocity both in the interview situation and in kin and non-kin components of French culture. This is in line with operational methods of anthropology. The give and take between me and the informant gave me important clues.[11] As this section will show, the insights from the interview situation eventually extended to a search for different styles of reciprocity in international relations. I learned about gift exchange because my informant and others in French culture, including Marcel Mauss, found the process useful as a personal means of perceiving the world and also as a framework for scientific research and interpretation.

First Stage: 1950-1952
The period of time covered by this study is almost ten years. In 1950 I completed undergraduate studies in anthropology at the University of California, concentrating on processes of cross-cultural communications and public policy formation. These interests derived from three years as

10. According to Lewis Coser, in introducing the concept of 'social conflict' in his preface to *The Functions of Social Conflict* (Glencoe, Ill.: Free Press, 1956), 'Concepts may be thought of as being neither true nor false; they are apt or inept, clear or vague, fruitful or useless. There are tools designed to capture relevant aspects of reality . . .' (p. 7).
11. I found that my experience matched considerably that of Rosalie H. Wax as described in her 'Reciprocity as a Field Technique', *Human Organization*, Vol. 11, No. 3 (Fall, 1952), p. 35.

18

a United States government official in Japan. There I worked closely with anthropologists and sociologists in adapting informational materials for a variety of Japanese audiences. Thus the communication of ideas about Western technology, science, political organization, social values, religious beliefs and aesthetics became a problem of understanding the cultural setting in which these ideas were received. Moreover, the task involved a search for the interpersonal and mass media channels through which social change and 'peace-loving' attitudes could be cultivated.

Having participated as a propagandist in the interplay between the American variant of Western civilization and the Japanese variant of Asian civilization, I naturally developed an interest in sociological studies. I left Berkeley for Columbia University to start graduate work in February 1951. In the Department of Social and Philosophical Foundations of Education at Teachers College, I found a congenial setting from which I could follow these interests. The late Prof. Lyman Bryson, also a member of the board of the Institute for Intercultural studies in New York, introduced me to the resources of the University and the city. Having written in *The Communication of Ideas* that the 'dominant intellectual tendency of our time . . . is to think more of processes and less of things,'[12] he helped me to plan a Ph.D. program, with anthropology at its base, in order to understand the processes of cultural transmission, and the diffusion of ideas across cultural boundaries. Courses taught by the late Dr. Alfred Kroeber and Dr. Margaret Mead were points of departure for a plan permitting me to study in Europe as part of my Columbia program.

This coincided with the growth of both governmental and scholarly concerns about how industrial nations might share techniques and knowledge with underdeveloped societies or nations. For example, Dr. Mead was editing *Cultural Patterns and Technical Change* for the World Federation of Mental Health.[13] With my arrival in Paris in June 1951 to study at the Institute of Ethnology, Musée de l'Homme, I was to find further evidence of UNESCO's interest in the social implications of technological change. Its new journal, *Impact,* was dedicated to stimulate studies along these lines. In such an intellectual climate, I was to follow my plan to shift my focus temporarily away from my own society and its policy orientations, and toward societies with tribal and village arrangements that would afford me a chance to see 'cultural wholes' and to observe the process of social change through new techniques and ideas. If French culture was to become a part of my study, it would be a by-product of a concentration on some African community in which the French may have

12. New York: Harper & Bros., 1948, p. 2.
13. First published in the UNESCO Tensions and Technology Series, 1953, and later, as a Mentor Book, in 1955.

come as administrators or missionaries. Thus I chose a Berber village, in consultation with French social scientists (the late Robert Montagne and Professor Louis Massignon), and started a study of the Berber language as preparation to do field work near Meknes, Morocco.

I was beginning to phrase questions I might ask of a pre-industrial people starting to use machinery: How do Berbers feel about giving up their camels for tractors? If the French are teaching the Berbers how to improve food production, what will the French need to know about the Berbers' religous and social life before they try to convince them they need tractors? How is social change introduced in a Moslem society, and how is change accepted or resisted? Who has participated in the planning of change? What customs, other than technology, are likely to be modified?

These questions were influenced, in part, by conversations with UNESCO social scientists, especially Alfred Métraux, who had worked on the preparation of the following UNESCO resolutions (3. 231 and 3. 24): 'To study possible methods of relieving tensions caused by the introduction of modern techniques in non-industrialized countries and those in the process of industrialization'; and 'To bring together and to diffuse existing knowledge and to encourage studies of the methods of harmonizing the introduction of modern technology in countries in process of industrialization, with respect for their cultural values so as to ensure the social progress of the peoples.'[14]

Two obstacles prevented my carrying out field work in Morocco: 1) difficulty in obtaining adequate skill in the Berber language in time to undertake the field work according to a schedule worked out with French authorities; and 2) failure to secure necessary funds for support during a six-month period in Morocco. Therefore I decided to postpone field work in a pre-literate, peasant or folk culture, and remain in France to continue an earlier interest in man in complex civilizations. This was influenced by some familiarity with the work of Dr. David Mandelbaum, especially his studies of sub-cultures in India described as a 'proper subject for anthropology' in 'The Study of Complex Civilizations,'[15] a paper by Dr. Conrad Arensberg on business civilization, read before the December 1949 meeting of the American Anthropological Association in Berkeley, and con-

14. Quoted by Margaret Mead in the foreword of *Cultural Patterns and Technical Change* (1953), p. 5.
15. Out of his own studies of sub-cultures in India, military organizations in the United States and studies by others, Dr. Mandelbaum wrote this essay for: WILLIAM L. THOMAS, Jr., ed. *Current Anthropology* (Chicago: University of Chicago Press, 1955), pp. 203-225.
16. Cf. MARGARET MEAD and RHODA MÉTRAUX, eds., *The Study of Cultures at a Distance* (Chicago: University of Chicago Press, 1953), and their *Themes in French Culture* (Stanford: Stanford University Press, 1954).

versations in New York with Dr. Margaret Mead about the work of Columbia University Research on Contemporary Cultures.[16] Moreover, Dr. Ruth Benedict's *Chrysanthemum and the Sword*, a product of her wartime work on contemporary cultures, had already proven a valuable guide to U.S. research and administrative efforts in Japan, and would become valuable to me again in cross-cultural comparisons of how people deal with gifts and obligations.

Second Stage: 1952-1956

A second effort to find a manageable focus for a study of technological change in a complex society came in November 1951. I was asked to serve as an English language tutor to a French engineer and owner of a small factory who was preparing to leave for the United States as chief of a productivity mission organized by the Marshall Plan to study American industrial practices. Payment for my language lessons was made in the form of food; that is, a student's fare in Paris was known to be poor, and I was invited to give my instruction during family luncheons. Thus an exchange relationship was established from the very start: food for knowledge, and later, knowledge for knowledge when the industrialist instructed me in French 'wisdom' about world politics, the communist threat in Islamic North Africa, and 'the dangers of idealism.'

Questions originally phrased for use in field work in Morocco became the tentative basis for both interviews and observations as I substituted a human group in France as my subject of study. Monsieur B., as the French engineer will be called, offered his cooperation in the study when I explained that I was trying to gather knowledge about the effects of the new technology on human relationships, and that my inquiry was related informally to studies being initiated by UNESCO. However, he saw our relationship as little affected by the fact that he would be supplying me with material about the inter-connections between the French institutions of family, religion, industry, and the state, and how these relationships might be changed by the new role he would soon play as a carrier of new technology. I was still perceived mainly as his language tutor, and he was consulting me, as an American friend, about life in the United States. Whatever I gathered in the way of information about him and his family, his workers, or his world view would come in the natural exchanges of friendship.[17] My having come to France to study the works of French

17. Daniel Lerner also has taken note of French expectations of reciprocity in the interview situation when he wrote: 'The insistence upon a highly participant interviewer – one who relieved the respondent's anxieties about "giving" by giving himself — gradually reshaped the basic formula of our interview.' See his 'Interviewing Frenchmen,' *The American Journal of Sociology*, Vol. LXII, No. 2 (September 1956),

scholars about the Berbers allowed him, moreover, to continue to see me as a young ethnologist primarily concerned with exotic people. The ethics of such an observer-observed relationship required me to remind him often that American social scientists, as well as my French colleagues at the Museum of Man, were increasingly interested in the behavior of modern man.

So I showed him an article from *Impact*, the UNESCO publication, in which the Dutch scholar, Professor R. J. Forbes of Amsterdam University, a historian of technology, wrote:

The transmission of ideas and techniques is not directly related to the mobility of man, to the development of communication. The resistence of 'recipients' and 'transmitters' of discoveries and inventions varies greatly. Such resistance is the direct result of the structure and fundamental principles of culture itself. Spiritual values may defer the acquisition of material achievements much longer than will the lack of technical knowledge. Still, research on this transmission, and into the question of where and when these new discoveries and inventions buttress or conflict with the 'receiving' civilization is sorely lacking in the history of technology.[18]

Thus in establishing clearly that our relationship was operating in several 'levels,' or that B. was playing several roles (English language pupil, French host, and informant), such written material became increasingly part of the method of the study. They served to remind B. that we were both trying to find out something about the nature of Western man. Moreover, Forbes' idea that 'spiritual values' might impede material progress appealed to B.'s belief that French technicians had a 'humanistic responsibility' to make 'man the master of the machine, and not the machine the master of man.' Here was an unexpected blending of 'method' and 'theory' and 'substantive data.' Written materials, first offered to clarify the observer-observed aspect of our relationship, acted as a projective technique.[19]

The interviews with B. were unstructured. The thought of introducing an 'artificial' instrument like a questionnaire would have been a source of

---

p. 194. I should make a distinction, however, between my role as a friend vis-à-vis my informant and the various less personal roles played by Lerner and his interview team members when they approached Frenchmen. Our experiences are similar in that we found Frenchmen interviewed prefer some *engagement* with the interviewer in contrast to talking to a 'response-recording machine.'

18. 'Technology and Society', *Impact*, Vol. 11, No. 1 (January-March 1950), p. 9.

19. 'The Battle Over Projective Techniques,' *Human Organization Clearinghouse Bulletin* (published by the Society for Applied Anthropology), Vol. III, No. 3 (1955), pp. 14-15. Cf. discussion of the personal interview and supplementary techniques in MURRAY WAX and L. J. SHAPIRO, 'Repeated Interviewing,' *The American Journal of Sociology*, Vol. LXII, No. 2 (September 1956), p. 215.

displeasure to my informant.[20] However, I consulted with the French public opinion institute, headed by Professor Jean Stoetzel, on several occasions to be kept informed of quantified research on French beliefs and attitudes on social and political questions. Similarly, I was granted permission to see once-classified or restricted U.S. government documents based on opinion studies done for American guidance in the conduct of Marshall Plan aid programs and the eventual development of the North Atlantic Treaty Organization military assistance scheme.[21] These materials gave me the opportunity to 'place' B. in the context of national 'trends' or 'averages' in beliefs held about, for example, the intentions or aims of the U.S. and the U.S.S.R. in Europe. At this stage of research, I was interested in the opportunity to be a participant-observer and to take notes of both verbal and other sets of behavior related to B.'s various roles as head of family and head of factory, as a former military officer and patriot, and as a Roman Catholic. My first ordering of incomplete data was influenced by Harold Lasswell's definition of the communication process as: Who Says What to Whom in What Channel with What Effect.[22] I saw B. as the audience, the 'to whom." What I was discovering about his worlds of family, worship, and work would have eventual relevance for the messages, techniques, or ideas he would obtain from his American experience.

The other elements in the communication process would be: a) United States government officials, industrialists, academicians, and trade unionists as the 'who,' the sources of ideas and techniques; b) their channels in reaching French productivity audiences (managers, government officials, and workers) would include books, films, lectures, pamphlets, and, above all, the 'team technique' of organizing groups of Frenchmen to visit the U.S. for six-week study periods; and c) the 'effects' of the communication, i.e., whether or not productivity was increased, whether the message was distorted or transformed in the process of going through various cultural filters, and whether changes in social behavior and attitudes could be detected over a period of time. Each phase of the process could constitute an elaborate study in itself. I decided to concentrate on B.'s life history as a case study of the 'to whom,' trying to understand him *in vivo* in the contexts of his family, factory, profession, class and national community.

20. DANIEL LERNER, 'Interviewing Frenchmen,' *The American Journal of Sociology*, Vol. LXII, No. 2 (September 1956), p. 188.
21. For example a study of H. PARRY and L. CRESPI, *Public Opinion in Western Europe* (Research Branch, Office of Special Representative in Europe, Paris, January, 1953), pp. 257 f.
22. See 'The Structure and Function of Communication in Society,' in LYMAN BRYSON, ed., *The Communication of Ideas* (New York: Harper, 1948), p. 37.

The first stage of the inquiry began in November 1951, when I first started seeing B. as his tutor, and continued at intervals until September 1952, when I returned to the United States. Approximately 100 interviews were put into notes, some in B.'s presence as we talked and many after my return to my own quarters. Observations were made at various places: the family apartment in Neuilly-sur-Seine, the factory in Puteaux, the conference rooms of the manufacturers' association, at Roman Catholic mass, during weekend visits to the family cottage outside of Paris, and at meetings of military reserve officers' association. Data were gathered before and after the mission's trip to the U.S.

When the team, consisting of fourteen persons, returned to France in March 1952, I conducted interviews with all the members and read their preliminary reports out of which a final report was to be made to Marshall Plan agencies in Paris. Extended interviews were repeated with individual members of the group in September 1954 and again in July and September 1956.[23] B., as head of the mission, remained my chief subject of attention as I was able to follow him on his daily rounds in Paris and at his ancestral village in Lorraine.

To arrive at cultural dimensions which affected French perceptions of American behavior and, by extension, their willingness to accept the U.S. as a model for an industrial society, I checked interview responses against the hypotheses of Geoffrey Gorer, Margaret Mead, and Rhoda Métraux in *Themes in French Culture*. Later, I did thematic analyses of thirty reports of productivity teams from other industries (paint and varnish, machine tools, etc.) to compare verbal with written descriptions of American culture, finding general congruence. A side interest in continuities and discontinuities in French cultural values led me to examine Alexis de Tocqueville's *Democracy in America*. This set of observations of American life, made in 1832, came strikingly close to those of the French productivity teams, suggesting not so much that U.S. life has remained the same as that the French structure their perceptions, and organize them, around fairly predictable themes.[24]

23. I kept to unstructured questions to find out, among other things, what salient themes might emerge from recall of their contacts with American people, particularly the meanings Frenchmen attached to the idea of productivity as explained by American managers and engineers. Cf. ROBERT K. MERTON, MARJORIE FISKE and PATRICIA KENDALL, *The Focused Interview* (Glencoe, Ill.: The Free Press, 1956), *passim*.

24. The four major cultural variables isolated from these combinations of interview responses and historical and contemporary written materials were: 1) *The French cult of food:* the behaviors associated with the marketing, preparation, serving, consumption and reflection on the quality of food as a source of pleasure beyond the satisfaction of visceral drives; 2) *French familism:* the behaviors associated with the beliefs, shared by persons in upper, middle, and working classes, that the *foyer*, the

Third Stage: 1956-1960

By 1956, when my wife and I returned to France to spend three months of field work, I was entering another stage of trying to 'grip the material in a satisfying way.'[25] I knew that I was returning to an environment where French social scientists with whom I might discuss my materials were influenced by Marcel Mauss. His lingering influence, expressed in research topics chosen by his former students,[26] had been rejuvenated by the publication in 1950 of his collected works in *Sociologie et Anthropologie*.[27] However, I had never seriously entertained the thought of applying Mauss' ideas to my own material, still in the process of being gathered. Instead, I was still equipped with such precedents of description and analysis as represented by studies of communication, interaction, learning, communities processes and cultural transmission.[28] Also, I was anticipating signs of French behavior that might reflect a phenomenon I had discussed with Dr. George Devereux, the anthropologist at the Menninger Foundation in 1950: the hostility felt by some people towards those they were imitating. Devereux called this 'antagonistic acculturation.'[29]

---

family household, is the individual's primary source of identification, prestige, and emotional satisfaction rather than jobs or professional achievement; 3) *Social class conflict:* the unsolved tensions or strains in French social structure involving the following elements in historical sequence: a) *Seigneurie* (altar and throne); b) Bourgeois, peasant proprietor, and deputy; and c) the industrial order with its internal conflicts between managerial and working groups; and 4) *Deductive and analytical intellectual processes:* the tendency to classify new experience, or communication content, according to principles or general statements which can be broken down into discrete components, and re-assembled to form a schematic which admittedly violates reality, but which is geometric, and therefore aesthetically pleasing, and a more efficient way of packaging, storing and delivering information. These variables became part of my effort to understand the cross-cultural communication process, namely, what facts about persons in the receiving culture are likely to affect the phrasing and transmissions of ideas and techniques. (Cf. DANIEL LERNER, 'Interviewing Frenchmen,' p. 190.)

25. JOHN DOLLARD, *Criteria for the Life History* (New Haven: Yale University Press, 1935), p. 1.

26. For example, the analytical study of exchanges of primitive money being done in 1953 by my colleague, Prof. Pierre Bessaignet, at Hobart and William Smith Colleges, where he introduced discussions of Mauss at departmental meetings.

27. C. LÉVI-STRAUSS, ed., *Sociologie et Anthropologie* (Paris: Presses Universitaires de France, 1950), pp. 145-279.

28. For example, I was interested in the possibility of finding the 'gatekeepers' encountered by my informant, B., in his industrial education by Americans. See the discussion of Kurt Lewin's 'channels' model by Bernard J. Siegel in 'Models for the Analysis of the Educative Process in American Communities,' in C. SPINDLER, ed., *Education and Anthropology* (Stanford: Stanford University Press, 1955), pp. 38-49.

29. Cf. G. DEVEREUX and E. LOEB, 'Antagonistic Acculturation,' *American Sociological Review*, Vol. VIII (April 1943), pp. 133-147. The phrase seemed to apply to

After a few weeks in France, I began to incorporate more seriously the ideas of both Mauss and Devereux into my collection of possible analytical tools for understanding both the older and newer materials from my study. As I shall explain below, Mauss' theory of gifts and obligations eventually gave me the most suitable framework for this exposition. Devereux's point about antagonistic acculturation was useful in keeping me attune to elements of hostility and ambivalence in French reactions to American teaching and giving. Lasswell's communications schema kept me reminded of flow or movement in a social process.

Thus several themes played contrapuntally in my mind as I observed behavior and noted what Frenchmen told me. I began to locate a pattern in the French lamentations about their war losses, economic weakness, political instability and complaints of outside interference in French affairs. New American statements (e.g., press releases from Marshall Plan headquarters) about the needs for helping France grow strong brought responses of self justification on the part of my French informants. Death statistics were often quoted from the two recent world wars and the Indo-China conflict ('Other nations could be more modern, prosperous and less dependent because they have suffered less.') Interlarded in these remarks were familiar characterizations of America as a nation of adolescents, playing dangerous games with powerful toys, or as the new Rome, turning Europe into one of its provinces. At first, I had taken such 'anti-American' statements in 1951, 1952 and 1954 as a sign of intimacy and acceptance. I presumed that my joking relationship with informants was a sign of rapport. In 1956, I began to see these statements as indicators of a more generalized feeling of obligation to a donor and frustration at not being able to discharge it. French notions of 'self' seemed integrally bound to identification with a nation whose humiliation had come through dependence on gifts and instruction from outsiders.

Such an interpretation developed in the following way. The 1956 field trip coincided with the threat felt by Frenchmen over the Suez crisis then developing. Interviews reflected even stronger than usual French complaints about American interference and naiveté. I sought explanations first from the findings of industrial sociology. How do people react to 'too much' supervision? What are predictable responses of people who have felt dependent 'too long?' What are the symptoms of people who have had their communications blocked? My questions were influenced by industrial and organizational studies as reported by Conrad M. Arensberg.[30]

---

the French case in view of the spontaneous anti-American remarks in my interviews with Frenchmen who were plainly dedicated to changing their manufacturing methods to fit some American practices.
30. See, for example, his 'Behavior and Organization: Industrial Studies,' in J.

I began to take a diagnostic view of the new data, being unable to concentrate on 'pure' description. Two French social scientists, Dr. Jean-Roger Herrenschmidt and Dr. Claude Tardits, hearing my verbal reports about the interviews, suggested that I might want to look at American aid to France as a form of potlatch. They were familiar with Ruth Benedict's use of Malinowski's Trobriand material and Boas' work on the Kwakiutls in her *Patterns of Culture*,[31] and, like most French social scientists, they were intimately familiar with the ideas of Mauss on gift exchange, particularly his treatment of the obligation to make countergifts. Moreover, both Herrenschmidt and Tardits had personal experience as 'cultural mediators' in the administration of Marshall Plan aid to France. Herrenschmidt, a former student of political science at Harvard, had written his Ph.D. dissertation on *Problems of Technical Assistance* (1954) and had briefed French productivity teams on American history and social institutions before their departure for the United States. Both felt, from the standpoint of personal experience and bi-cultural views based on U.S. and French sociology, that the French were suffering from the humiliation of gifts and that there existed no means yet for their countrymen to restore self-esteem by 'returning the gift.'

Lasswell's communications schema remained in mind as I took the cue about gifts from the French social scientist. Thus in reviewing *Essai sur le don*, and the literature on which Mauss based some of his analyses of reciprocity, I began to see analogues in the processes of communicating ideas and the giving of gifts. There were givers or senders in both processes, and there were receivers who responded 'with some effect.' What was the effect? Did the receiver send back a message or a gift? If so, what kind of message or gift? Communications engineers spoke of 'feedback'[32]. Were there any analogues in French reponses to American giving and teaching? What were the French 'feeding back' to Americans? Statements of gratitude? Resentment? Why?

With such free association, I found that earlier studies of communica-

---

ROHRER and M. SHERIF, eds., *Social Psychology at the Crossroads* (New York: Harper & Bros., 1951), pp. 324-352.

31. Boston: Houghton Mifflin Co., 1934.

32. Three personal experiences laid the groundwork for my interest in electronics as a suggestive model for studying social processes: 1) wartime training as a radio mechanic, and later as a cryptography instructor, in which duties I first had to learn to read a schematic and build electrical circuits, and then send and receive coded and decoded messages through devices similar to those we had constructed – a valuable rehearsal for any thinking about structure and process; 2) hearing a 1949 lecture in Berkeley by Dr. Norbert Weiner on 'Feedback,' in which principles of cybernetics were explained to an audience of physicists, social scientists, and a few poets – an event responsible for considerable campus discussion of the human implications of

27

tions contributed to an understanding of giving, receiving and repaying as a circular process. By thinking of gifts as analogous to messages, I started to look back over my old materials to trace the idea of productivity through its various communications networks. Following the circulation of an idea was to prove a useful preparation for comprehending structure and process as represented by Malinowski's description of the movement and countermovement of ceremonial objects in the *kula* ring. I was discovering, for myself, some aspects of the anthropological tradition of comparing human groups. Could I find similar processes at work among a group of French recipients of American gifts, a group of South Sea chiefs and fishermen, and industrial workers in Chicago?[33] Once able to think that gifts might be analogues of messages sent abroad and received, my next step was to reconsider the social relationships between donors and receivers. In this way, I began the third stage of this study, 1956-1960. I was tempted at first to try a synthesis of theories about interaction, communications, and gift exchange relationships, but settled temporarily on gift behavior as a more manageable framework within which to organize and present my findings.

Subsequent experience has reinforced my belief that we need more knowledge about how social relationships are affected by gifts, and that such knowledge has important implications for the conduct of daily life and foreign affairs. As an officer of a small philanthropic foundation since 1957, I have had opportunity to participate in a number of donor-receiver relationships in which I have been reminded of the relevance of Mauss' theory of obligation in yet another context. (Foundation giving in the United States would offer rich materials for analysis of American cultural devices for dealing with feelings of indebtedness to donors.) Also, two brief visits to West Africa in 1959 and 1960, permitting me informal inquiries into institutionalized reciprocity, or the lack of it, in the 'colonial situation,' have given me further impetus to pursue this study of technical assistance as a form of a gift exchange.

The preceding section describes the natural history of the study, including the methods, materials, and concepts which helped me discover

---

studying electronic devices; and 3) finding these two previous experiences pertinent, in 1951, in Paris, when I tried to understand a lecture on cybernetics by Prof. Claude Lévi-Strauss, the ethnologist, who saw possibilities for intellectual collaboration of persons in the human and physical sciences. With further reading of Percy Bridgman's *The Logic of Modern Physics* (New York: Macmillan, 1928), especially his discussion of photographic tracing of electrons, I still refer to my tactile knowledge of tracing the flow of electrical currents and radio messages when drawing diagrams of circulation of gifts in interpersonal networks.

33. See discussion of industrial sociology in Chapter IV.

the usefulness of Marcel Mauss' theory of gift exchange as a framework for presenting a case study of international technical assistance.[34] Now let us turn to a brief interpretation of Mauss in the recent history of French sociology and a statement of his relevance to this particular study.

C. THE SIGNIFICANCE OF MARCEL MAUSS FOR THIS STUDY

The significance of Marcel Mauss for understanding neglected reciprocal aspects of technical assistance processes will emerge, I hope, in the unfolding of the data and interpretations in this study. First, however, I want to summarize at least three contributions of Mauss' studies of gifts as they bear on this presentation:

1) Mauss' insistence on studies of concrete, observable phenomena as a means to understand a whole system of social life;

2) Mauss' example as a student and practitioner of the comparative method in sociology; and

3) His reminder that old human problems turn up in new guises. As a student in Paris, listening to lectures by Mauss' interpreter and successor, Lévi-Strauss, I used to hear references to Mauss' admonition, to the previous generation of students, that they could analyze all of Hopi culture by starting with a prayer feather. Students were told how to trace interconnections between the feather and other material and non-material aspects of Hopi life: religious beliefs and practices, kinship and social structure, techniques of art and agriculture, etc. Such advice stuck in my mind as I approached the materials of this study and discovered that a set of gestures words, and movements of one informant, considered as a microcosm, could be a concrete manifestation of a much larger order of international events. B. then became for me one instance in a larger case of French-American relations during the Marshall Plan and subsequent efforts to weld culturally diverse people into a mutual security system.

In his essay on the gift, Mauss wrote:

The study of the concrete, which is the study of the whole, is made more readily, is more interesting and furnishes more explanations in the sphere of sociology than the study of the abstract. For we observe complete and complex beings. We too describe them in their organisms and *psychai* as well as their behavior in groups, with the attendant psychoses: sentiments, ideas and desires

---

34. On the process of discovery, see C. WRIGHT MILLS' essay, 'On intellectual Craftsmanship,' in L. GROSS, ed., *Symposium on Sociological Theory* (Evanston and White Plains: Row, Peterson & Co., 1959), p. 51, in which he advised sociologists: 'Make your context of presentation reveal your context of discovery.'

of the crowd, of organized societies and their sub-groups. We see bodies and their reactions, and their ideas and sentiments as interpretations or as motive forces. The aim and principle of sociology is to observe and understand the whole group in its total behavior.[35]

I have already mentioned in this introduction the comparative method used by Mauss in analyzing the *kula* ring as described by Malinowski. The full range of his comparisons, of course, goes far beyond Malinowski's materials. Prof. E. E. Evans-Pritchard, in his introduction to the English translation of *The Gift*, praised Mauss' work as a masterpiece of the comparative method of sociology, and went on to elaborate:

Mauss shows in this essay what is the real nature, and what is the fundamental significance, of such institutions as the *potlatch* and the *kula* which at first sight bewilder us or even seem to be pointless and unintelligible. And when he shows us how to understand them he reveals not only the meaning of customs of North American Indians and of Melanesians but at the same time the meaning of customs in the early phases of historical civilizations; and, what is more, the significance of practices in our own society at the present time. In Mauss' essays there is always implicit a comparison, or contrast, between the archaic institutions . . . and our own.[36]

Evans-Pritchard's evaluation of Mauss' attention to contemporary societies through the comparative method leads naturally into the third contribution of Mauss to this study, namely, his reminder that old problems are turning up in new guises. Mauss has ended his scholarly career before the Marshall Plan, and died the year before the field work for this study started. I should like to think that Mauss would have found familiar principles of gift exchange operating inside various contemporary international efforts to distribute goods and ideas. I have concentrated on the Marshall Plan prelude to the North Atlantic Treaty Organization. The obligations he found in earlier and pre-literate societies might also be discovered motivating and activating the behavior of donors and recipients who make up other technical assistance efforts: the Colombo Plan, United Nations aid to the Congo, assistance given by the Soviet Union to China and East European nations; the help offered by Israel to Ghana; or the 'co-prosperity' gifts of the post-war Japanese to Algeria and India.

Taking us to the threshold of his own personal observations of reciprocity at work in complex civilizations, Mauss was unable to go further than to leave a rich intellectual legacy of concepts and an analytical method for his survivors to apply empirically today. His essay on gifts appeared

35. *The Gift: Forms and Functions of Exchange in Archaic Societies,* English translation by I. Cunnison (Glencoe, Ill.: Free Press, 1954), p. 78. The word *psychai* appears in italics in both Cunnison's translation and Mauss' original essay.
36. *Ibid.,* p. ix.

at mid-point in his intellectual career in 1925 when Europe was enjoying an equilibrium between the two world wars. It can be assumed that his projected works on prayer, on money, and on the state, which were never completed, would have dealt with reciprocity between man and gods, reciprocity as it relates to the exchange of money in markets, and reciprocity as it explains the relationships between citizens and their civil servants.

Mauss' death in 1950 came after a long period of decline in his scholarly work. As Evans-Pritchard explains in his introduction to Cunnison's translation of *The Gift*, 'Paris was occupied by the Nazis, and Mauss was a Jew. He was himself not injured, but some of his closest colleagues and friends, Maurice Halbwachs and others, were killed. For the second time he saw all around him collapse, and this, combined with other and personal troubles, was too much for him and his mind gave way.'[37] Thus the extension of his work was left to the younger generation, especially Lévi-Strauss, who took inspiration from Mauss in his analysis of incest rules and kinship structures in *Les structures élémentaires de la parenté*.[38] Another member of the younger generation to use Mauss' ideas, in this instance to understand relationships between contemporary nations, empires and alliances, is the French economist and philosopher, François Perroux.[39]

How does Mauss' treatment of gifts and their social setting fit into his general scholarly preoccupations? Not only as Durkheim's nephew but as his intellectual heir, Mauss fitted into the philosophical orientation of French savants. His forerunners, as were Durkheim's, included Montesquieu, Turgot, Condorcet, St. Simon, and Comte. This was a tradition, embellished by Durkheim, 'in which conclusions were reached by analysis of concepts rather than of facts, the facts being used as illustrations of formulations reached by other than inductive methods.' However, Mauss had access to anthropological field work which Durkheim lacked. The result is a scholarly method – a combination of factual and conceptual analysis – which Lévi-Straus has characterized:

Durkheim belongs definitely to the past, while Mauss is, still now, on the level of the more modern anthropological thought and research ... While he is often obscure by the constant use of antitheses, short-cuts and apparent paradoxes which, later on, prove to be the result of a deeper insight, he gratifies his listener, suddenly, with fulgurating intuitions ... one feels that one has reached the bottom of social phenomenon and 'hit the bed rock'. This constant striving toward the fundamental, this willingness to sift over and over again, a

37. *Ibid.*, p. vi.
38. Paris: Presses Universitaires de France, 1949, pp. xiv + 638 (2nd ed.: Paris/The Hague, Mouton, 1967).
39. See *L'Europe sans Rivages* (Paris: Presses Universitaires de France, 1954).

huge mass of data until the purest material only remains, explains Mauss' preference for the essay over the book, and the limited size of his published work.[40]

His essay on the gift is a particular example of such a fact-sifting process which also is represented in his other works, written in collaboration with Durkheim, Hubert and Beuchat: *Essai sur la nature et la fonction du sacrifice* (1899), *De quelques formes primitives de classification: contribution à l'étude des représentations collectives (1903), Esquisse d'une théorie générale de la magie* (1904), and *Essai sur les variations saisonnières des sociétés eskimos: essai de morphologie sociale* (1906).

Lowie, in describing French sociology in his *History of Ethnological Theory*, takes note of Mauss' scholarly style:

It had been one of Durkheim's favorite ideas ... to stress the quality of the documentation rather than the number of societies compared. 'The essential thing,' he wrote, 'is to unite not many facts, but facts at once typical and well studied.' This admirable principle guides Mauss in his study of primitive gifts no less than his earlier essay on Eskimo seasonalism.[41]

Thus Mauss, whether dealing with magic, sacrifice, collective behavior or gifts, had an interest in intensive documentation to produce concepts that might be useful in interpreting still wider and more complex sets of data. His scientific interest in classification shows through in all his works. But it is in his essay on Eskimo seasonalism and his essay on the gift that we find an equally important characteristic: the search for inter-relationships between phenomena. In his study of Eskimo life, he correlated economic aspects (caribou hunting and the quest for sea mammals) with social and religious life. Similarly, his classic on gifts provides a clear example of his search to see relationships between all the components of a culture: *les faits sociaux totaux*. 'Economic' facts normally confined to markets or exchanges of goods become meaningful only if shown in their total setting: juridical, religious, mythological, aesthetic, and moral.

Showing interdependence between the components or the building blocks of a society is by no means a novel idea or method among the structuralist-functionalist circle of Anglo-American social scientists today.[42] Mauss' analysis of human relationships influenced by exchange of gifts, however, remains an important model for examining action or movement within a social system, as well as in examining the process by which

40. See 'French Sociology,' in G. GURVITCH and W. MOORE, eds., *Twentieth Century Sociology* (New York: Philosophical Library, 1945), p. 52.
41. New York: Rinehart & Co., 1937, p. 215.
42. In his introduction to Mauss' essays, Lévi-Strauss (*Sociologie et Anthropologie*, p. x) shows parallels between Mauss's work and British and American 'schools,'

human organization grows out of reciprocities between individuals of the same or differing ranks.

By concentrating on both psychic and structural phenomena, Mauss avoided a completely static approach to interpreting social groups. His contribution to the understanding of reciprocity as a basis for social life is recognized, for example, in a recent essay (1959) by Alvin Gouldner, 'Reciprocity and Autonomy in Functional Theory.' Gouldner recommends readers to undertake research on reciprocal behavior and its structural contexts and to re-examine 'the principle of functional reciprocity as variously employed by Marx, Mauss, Malinowski, Lévi-Strauss, and Homans.'[43]

With the above brief suggestions of Mauss' significance for this study, I now wish to introduce a schematic summary of some of the dates and a preview of the interpretations which follow. The hope is that the reader will have a whole view of events and their sequences against which to interpret more detailed subsequent discussion of the obligations of giving, receiving, and repaying. B. should be visualized as standing at the center of an ever widening series of concentric circles representing his kin, community, and state relationships. The events in the larger community, including Indo-China, North Africa, and the United States, are shown not as a complete history of the 1950's, but as part of the geopolitical macrocosm reflected by B. at the moments of my interviews with him. Thus I am presenting a 'history within a history'[44] in order to give new meaning to Mauss' proposition that 'l'étude du concret qui est du complet, est possible et plus captivante et plus explicative encore en sociologie'[45] – his admoniton that the study of the concrete is the study of the whole.

---

mentioning as those who knew of Mauss through word-of-mouth and his then scattered essays: Radcliffe-Brown, Malinowski, Evans-Pritchard, Firth, Herskovits, Lloyd Warner, Redfield, Kluckhohn, Elkin, Held, etc. Mauss' 'modernism,' says Lévi-Strauss, led him to interests in psychosomatic medicine, the notion of homeostasis from the work of W. B. Cannon, and a fascination with the idea of communication of meanings by the movements of the body, especially in the training of reflexes of humans in their early childhood. His essay, 'Les techniques du corps,' appearing in the collected works, is a concrete example of this interest, and reflects Mauss' preoccupation with 'l'école anthropologique américaine, telle qu'elle allait s'exprimer dans les travaux de Ruth Benedict, Margaret Mead, et de la plupart des ethnologues américains de la jeune génération' (p. xi).

43. In L. GROSS, ed., *Symposium on Sociological Theory* (Evanston and White Plains: Row, Peterson & Co., 1959), pp. 248-251.

44. I owe this phrase to Sidney W. Mintz after his summary chapter in *Worker in the Canoe: A Puerto Rican Life History* (New Haven: Yale University Press, 1960), pp. 253-270.

45. 'Essai sur le don,' in C. LÉVI-STRAUSS, *Sociologie et Anthropologie*, p. 276.

D. THE FRENCH QUEST FOR AUTONOMY AND RECIPROCITY: A SCHEMATIC SUMMARY OF SOME OF THE DATA AND INTERPRETATIONS OF THIS STUDY

1. *Historical Background:*

EVENTS

June 5, 1947: General Marshall announces aid plan at Harvard University commencement.

November 7, 1947: Ambassador Harriman releases committee report, 'European Recovery and American Aid.'

March 31, 1948: 80th Congress appropriates 577 million dollars.

1948-1949: American food and tools offered to Europeans as first phase of aid program.

1949-50: Technical and managerial knowledge offered by U.S. Productivity teams organized to visit U.S. to study manufacturing processes.

January 1951: General Eisenhower makes tour of inspection of European military defenses in new role as commander of supreme headquarters of allied powers in Europe.

INTERPRETATION

These events are manifestations of the obligation Americans felt to give a share of their capital and intellectual goods to Europeans. U.S. initiated action, but consulted with Europeans on economic needs. Europeans invited to plan aid priorities, make some financial contribution in local currency, and device new government and industrial organization to encourage wise distribution of gifts of both tangible and intangible nature.

U.S. thus took on new role as benefactor-teacher nation; neglected to point out 'self-interest' aspects of aid. Gifts accompanied by advice to integrate Europe both politically and economically.

With military integration of Europe now being pressed by Americans, Europeans, especially the French, begin to feel new threats to independence. Eisenhower's presence, despite personal popularity, becomes symbol of U.S. as protector-benefactor-teacher nation. General de Gaulle becomes symbol of French resistance to France's acceptance of satellite status vis-à-vis U.S.

2. *Interpretation of the Interview Situations as a Microcosm of Franco-American Exchange Relationships: 1951-1960*

THE MACROCOSM

External Events, Trends Reflecting Donor-Teacher Role of United States vis-à-vis Receiver-Pupil Role of France.

THE MICROCOSM

Situations in which B. Responds to External Events in Interaction with American Teacher-Investigator.

November 1951: Korean and Indo-China wars dramatize Euro-American negotiations about mutual defense to prevent growth of Communism. French resist implications that defense requires German participation in Atlantic-nation pact. U.S. aid continues to France as keystone of defense effort. Frenchmen and other Europeans leaving for study in U.S. factories: then returning to transmit new knowledge to industries, government, and universities.

Monsieur B. appointed as chief of rubber industry productivity mission to U.S., finds American student of anthropology to serve as English language tutor in preparation for voyage.

B. tells tutor their age difference corresponds to international situation: France, the older, now having to learn from America, the younger; blames role reversal on French weakness from war, destruction, and death; asks Americans to listen to French wisdom about North African affairs to avoid youthful mistakes and naiveté as NATO defense efforts extend to Morocco. Informant-pupil offers food in exchange for English instruction.

January 1952: Indo-China war reduces imports of raw rubber to French industry as one of various indicators of disturbance in French economy and productive capacity.

B. Complains that Americans are latecomers to Asian battles; despite Korean war, U.S. should sympathize more with French effort in Indo-China; interviews give B. a chance to start 'up-the-line communication' with the American protector-donor, personified by tutor.

B. departs for U.S. January 9, 1952, stating that mission will help strengthen France's value to West-

March 1952: Despite domestic political unrest, the French continue the Indo-China war, watch warily the development of nationalist parties in North Africa, and keep up a flow of French industrialists, managers, and workers going to the U.S. and returning.

August 1952: Eisenhower's return to United States from France to accept Republican Party nomination for presidency.

ern world; insists that French living standards do not need to match American standards in order to keep a superior quality of civilization.

Six weeks pass in U.S., with team returning to digest their observations and findings in written reports. Frenchmen start codification of discrete pieces of U.S. knowledge and information about productivity practices, claiming that Americans are poor teachers, know little about principles of mass production, could speak only with examples, not general ideas. Finished reports amount to a French-style (Cartesian) analysis of U.S. economy. Gift of knowledge about organizing man's work and machines to produce more goods (at lower prices) begins circulation in France. B. makes speeches.

French value American experience in 'human relations' (management practices), hope they can put techniques (public relations, suggestion boxes) to use in France to reduce social class conflict, make industry productive enough to make up for strength lost through political instability. But French remain ambivalent about U.S. generosity; complain Americans asked them nothing in return for knowledge given (e.g., results of French scientific research and experiments in synthetics). B. offers tutor money to extend stay to continue studies in France, all the time reminding him of necessity of French to in-

Spring 1954: M. Bidault proclaims France a world power with important European, Atlantic, African and Asian interest; builds foreign policy on this assumption in negotiating with Government of Viet Nam for a reluctant transfer of sovereignty during Indo-China war. Frenchmen criticize 'concesssions' to Viet Nam as sign of French subservience to U.S. United States financing Indo-China war. France plays a game of power politics based on resources of others. U.S. impatiently waits for recompense for aid to Indo-China war in form of French ratification of European Defense Community pact originally proposed then abandoned by France.

Autumn 1954: Dien Bien Phu battle and French defeat produces new demoralization in France. Loss of prestige accompanied by new demands to resist U.S. efforts to persuade France to join supra-national organization (E.D.C.).

1955: France originates pressures on U.S. to take part in Geneva summit conference, finally attended by Faure, Eisenhower, Khrushchev, etc. Apart from diplomatic initiative, France takes lead in domestic debates on educational reform in France. Educators seek revisions in curricula to reflect new technology, manpower, requirements emerging from increased productivity.

October 1956: France, Britain and Israel act independently in Suez without informing U.S. Americans struct Americans to beware of mistakes in dealing with North African nationalists. With new administration ahead in U.S., Americans need help in dealing with a part of the world the French know better.

B. writes letters to New York urging American tutor to remember that France alone had been bearing brunt of resistance to Asian Communists; Korea a much shorter war.

He warns tutor that the West must negotiate from strength. That the U.S. was making France look soft by its dangerously idealistic 'anti-colonialism.'

In Paris interviews, September 1954, B. again reflects malaise over French defeat, shock at Algerian uprising; states that only de Gaulle can restore direction and dignity in France; remembers de Gaulle's 'humiliation' at hands of Roosevelt; FDR perceived as symbol of dangerous idealism, and man of power who would force French compliance in exchange for U.S. wartime aid. Anti-American feelings, however, did not interfere with B.'s desire to return to U.S., to send more technicians to U.S. for training.

B. writes that U.S. ought to share atomic knowledge with France; education of scientists throughout Occident needed to meet Communist threat; says U.S. not completely generous, too selective with gifts.

complain of ingratitude; Atlantic alliance threatened with dissolution. Suez crisis accompanied by renewed warnings to U.S. to beware of communist infiltration in Islamic Africa, reminders that West cannot afford to appease a 'new Hitler.'

June 1, 1958: De Gaulle returns to power; Algerian war continues; France prospers from productivity improvements, but faces uncertain future with war losses and precarious reform of political system.

February 13, 1960: French explode atomic device in Sahara and enter 'atomic club'; U.S., sensitive to black African reactions against French, show unenthusiastic response.

B., first in interviews and later in letters, shows new fury against U.S. efforts to frustrate French action; also enjoys elation that France could act once again without supervision, and in defiance of American benefactor; march into Suez regarded by B. as a dramatic, if drastic, means of forcing Americans to accept French 'gift' of political instruction. Suez serves as a catharsis, giving informant and other Frenchmen new feeling of autonomy, self-respect, control over own affairs.

December 9, 1958: B., in interview, expresses jubilance over de Gaulle's return; says U.S. will now have to deal with France as an equal partner, especially now that France, once refused atomic secrets by the U.S., is going ahead with research on atomic bomb; France 'paying back' U.S. with proofs of strength and genius which U.S. failed to recognize as valuable counter-gifts for earlier aid.

March 6, 1960: B. accuses, in interview, U.S. of jealousy over French success with bomb; de Gaulle, he says, will show Americans how to deal with Algerians and Russians; U.S. should be grateful to France for proving to U.S.S.R. that France is not a colony of U.S.

CHAPTER II

THE OBLIGATION TO GIVE

A. THE MOTIVES OF DONORS

In his analysis of exchange institutions among Polynesians, Melanesians, and Northwest Coast American Indians, Marcel Mauss developed a scientific and moral interest in a general theory of obligation.[1] He found, by studying results of fieldwork in a variety of pre-literate societies, what he believed to be one of the bases of social life[2] which embraces a large part of humanity over a long transitional phase and persists 'in this day among peoples other than those described.'[3] He referred to the institutions and practices making up a kind of social and psychological pattern.[4] The pattern consists of rights and duties through which people feel obliged to give, to receive, and to repay gifts of both tangible and intangible nature. Mauss wrote:

Food, women, children, possessions, charms, land, labor, services, religious offices, rank – *everything is stuff to be given away and repaid* [Italics mine]. In the perpetual interchange of what we may call spiritual matter, comprising men and things, these elements pass and repass between clans and individuals, ranks, sexes and generations.[5]

In this chapter, attention will be focused on the first of the three obligations mentioned by Mauss, the obligation to give. With this abstraction as a working tool, let us examine some of the elements of the giving process,

1. Derived from the Latin word *obligatus*, obligation is variously defended as 'a binding requirement as to action; duty: *to fulfill every obligation* ... the binding power or force of a promise, law, duty, agreement, etc., ... a benefit, favor, or service for which gratitude is due ... the state or fact of being indebted for a benefit, favor, or service.' See CLARENCE L. BARNHART, ed., *The American College Dictionary* (New York and London: Harper & Bros., 1948).
2. M. MAUSS, *The Gift*, p. 2.
3. *Ibid.*, p. 45.
4. *Ibid.*, p. 11.
5. *Ibid.*, p. 12.

as one 'human universal'[6] in the light of fieldwork done on French and American exchange relationship during the period under study, 1951-1960.

Three questions, at least, are pertinent to this analysis of the obligation to give: 1) Why do people offer gifts? 2) What can the offering of a gift tell us about the rank of the donor or the social relationships within which gifts are given?[7] 3) Can knowledge, considered as a gift, become part of a nation's obligation to give? I will suggest answers to these questions by illustrating statements by Mauss and other students of pre-literate and historical peoples by brief descriptions of the United States' role as a donor nation vis-à-vis the French during the period of relationships as influenced by the Marshall Plan and the North Atlantic Treaty Organization.

Mauss states that many people make generous offers of gifts and that these gifts seem to be offered voluntarily, disinterestedly, and spontaneously. The social position of the donor, however, and the 'inherent' principle of making return gifts require the student of gift exchange to realize that the behavior accompanying the gift is 'formal pretence and social deception,' while the transaction itself is based on obligation and economic self-interest.[8] Mauss recognizes that gift-giving may take various forms and, for both individuals and groups, represents a mixture of motives. Rules

6. See *Outline of Cultural Materials* (3rd rev. ed.; New Haven: Human Relations Area Files, Inc., 1950), which lists 'gift-giving' as the first of nine types of mechanisms of transferring economic goods and the titles to them. Gift-giving is a category of human activity defined and then classified under sub-headings in the following manner: 'Alienation of property by gift; rights, privileges, and powers of donor and recipient; frequency, types, occasions and purposes of gifts, social relationships within which gifts are given; formalities of giving and receiving; potlatches; reciprocal gift exchange (e.g., *kula*); role of gifts in the distribution of economic goods, etc.' See section on 'Exchange,' p. 54.

7. I am phrasing such questions as a preliminary to a more systematic analysis, to be done outside of this study, of the situational and relational aspects of gift exchange in a variety of cultural contexts. Obviously, for example, the first question fails to take into immediate account the great range of cultural variation possible in the motives of donors. The second question, moreover, does not even speculate on the fascinating number of possible types of social structure (superordinate-subordinate relations, egalitarism or peer relationships) within which persons can initiate gifts or respond to gifts. A more complex consideration deals with the need to specify gift behavior growing out of both cross-cultural and intra-cultural exchanges. See, for example, the brief comparison between a child's birthday party in the United States and aspects of the *vartan bhanji* mechanism of gift exchange in the Punjab in Zekiye Eglar's *A Punjabi Village in Pakistan* (New York: Columbia University Press, 1960), p. 127. A useful theoretical framework within which to consider such examples is Gregory Bateson's essay, 'Formulation of End Linkage' in M. MEAD and R. MÉTRAUX, eds., *The Study of Culture at a Distance* (Chicago: University of Chicago Press, 1953), especially his discussion of dominance-submission, exhibitionism-spectatorship, and succoring-dependence motifs as expressed variously in relationships between high and low status individuals or groups, pp. 374-378.

of generosity are widespread, however.[9] Recognizing the social sanctions and self-interest motives which keep gifts in circulation, Mauss suggests implicitly that human groups (clans, tribes, families), through individuals[10] who represent these groups, seek various satisfaction by being donor.[11] Among these are: a) feeling of doing religious duties; b) prestige and peace; and c) expectation of return gifts.

1. Giving and Religious Obligation

Mauss approached religious duties related to gift-giving by references to North-East Siberian and West Alaskan Eskimo societies as examples of 'the theme of the economy and morality of the gift: that of the gift made to men in the sight of gods or nature.'[12] A description of these and other religious practices led Mauss to a beginning of theories of both sacrifice and alms, both related to gifts, in which primitive religions, Hinduism, Buddhism, and the Judaeo-Christian and Islamic traditions encourage people to give. Without generosity, Mauss wrote, Nemesis 'will take vengeance upon excessive wealth and happiness of the rich by giving to

8. MAUSS, *The Gift*, p. 1.

9. *Ibid.*, p. 17.

10. Mauss fails to show the steps necessary to link individual and collective phenomena, either in a small society made up of face-to-face relationships, or in more complex societies where an individual's identification with the larger group may come about through exposure to shared symbols (flags, totems, or public figures on a television screen). Nevertheless, Mauss is relevant to understanding parallels between a small group of Trobriand wives and children waving goodbyes to husbands and fathers as they sail on a *kula* expedition, and Americans who follow, by newspapers and television, their president as he leaves for state visits and both gives and receives symbolic gifts. Ceremonial gift exchange between heads of state may be residues of earlier points in time when such gifts were more meaningful to the whole public than now. A carpet from the Shah of Iran to the President of the United States, or a hydro-jet cabin cruiser built as an American gift to Premier Khrushchev, but withdrawn after the cancellation of President Eisenhower's June 10, 1960, trip to Moscow, are examples of how individual citizens may 'participate' in international gift exchange through intermediaries who are both giving and receiving. The actual exchanges themselves may be overshadowed by geopolitical concerns (e.g. Middle East oil or the Berlin crisis), but they are concrete reminders of the universality of gifts as important elements in building steady relationships, satisfying the prestige of donors and receivers, and expressing collectively what can be felt individually.

11. Another satisfaction which might be added is gregariousness or sociability, the pleasure of contact with other people. The point about gregariousness is made with two things in mind: a) Mauss' descriptions of courtesies, entertainment, dances, feasts, and fairs (cf. MAUSS, *The Gift*, p. 3); and b) an analysis of social contact and isolation by Kingsley Davis in his *Human Society* (New York: Macmillan, 1950), see especially Ch. VI, 'Forms of Interaction,' pp. 147-171.

12. MAUSS, *The Gift*, p. 12.

the poor and the gods. The gods and spirits consent that the portion reserved for them and destroyed in useless sacrifice should go to the poor and the children.'[13] Not only the recipient but the donor also becomes the beneficiary of such gifts. He is 'rewarded' in the sight of God, or gods, by carrying out his religious duties.

So it is with the United States as one of the modern nations in which the Judaeo-Christian tradition influences the choices (i.e., values) of secular legislators, taxpayers, and administrators in offering gifts of technical assistance to 'less favored' nations.[14] Writing on 'Christian Faith and Technical Assistance,' Margaret Mead recognized the historical importance of religion in stimulating gifts to the advantage of the donor:[15]

Throughout the last two thousand years, Christianity and Judaism have provided the religious ethic which gave meaning and purpose to the attempts to ease the misery and lighten the darkness of the slave, the serf, the peasant, the heathen, and the aboriginal inhabitants of the newly discovered continents and islands beyond the sea. In the Judaic ethic, to heal, to teach, and to feed the poor were good deeds, *benefiting the giver, in fact benefiting the giver to such a degree that the recipient was hardly expected to reciprocate with more than moral deference* [italics mine]. Similarly, in traditional Christianity the care of the sick, teaching the ignorant, and feeding the hungry were all works through which individuals, acting in Christian compassion and charity, walked more closely in the ways of the Lord.[16]

While Mead thus set the broad historical stage for religious motives behind technical assistance programs, another student of U.S. foreign aid also brings to mind Mauss' point about the widespread 'theme of the economy and morality of the gift.' Eric Larrabee, a social historian interested in the decline of the Protestant ethic in American culture and the secularizing of puritan values in industrial societies, wrote:

... What is characteristically American about Point IV (of President Truman's inaugural speech) is the institutionalized zeal with which it embodies a con-

13. *Ibid.*, pp. 15-16.
14. It is the task of another study than this one to analyze the religious and moral justifications used by foreign aid proponent in the U.S. government. An interesting comparison could be made between, say, American, Japanese, Israeli, British, and Egyptian appeals to religious (i.e., Christian, Buddhist, Hebrew, Moslem, and Shinto) duty or moral law as justification for public spending on behalf of poorer nations.
15. I have not studied Northern European and Mediterranean variants of Christian notions of giving. A clue from which students of European sub-cultures might start, however, is a reference to Calvinist understanding of obligations and charity in L. MUMFORD, *The Condition of Man* (New York: Harcourt, Brace & Co., 1944), pp. 192-193.
16. See her essay in W. H. COWAN, ed., *What the Christian Hopes for in Society* (New York: Association Press, 1957), pp. 81-82.

viction – verging on the theological – in the perfectibility of mankind's material well-being ... There is nothing exclusively American about the rudiments of Christian charity which show themselves in awareness by the privileged of the plight of the less privileged, or about the blended compassion an arrogance that show themselves in Christian evangelism ... the situation favored a peculiar blend of materialistic and missionary motives.[17]

In these observations of religion and technical assistance, we find indirect support for Mauss' proposition that donors give gifts out of obligation and self-interest. These are by no means complete answers to the question, 'Why do people offer gifts?' However, they serve my immediate aim: to suggest similarities in the mixed economic and religious motives of preliterate people and modern industrial people in their felt obligation to give. They suggest that a case can be made for the notion that the 'pure gift' – the disinterested act of generosity – is rarely, if ever, found in human societies, regardless of religious ideals exalting the free gift (e.g., the Christian concept of grace). The United States' Marshall Plan aid to France would be an example of such a religiously and economically motivated gift in the modern world.[18]

2. Giving for Prestige and Peace

Prestige, as an American goal in itself, was not to enter public discourse to any explicit degree until the advent of the presidential campaign in

17. See his essay 'Changing American Attitudes Toward Point IV,' *Confluence*, Vol. IV, No. 4 (January 1956), p. 460. In this essay, Larrabee also observed that 'if President Truman was acute in perceiving that a usable residue of Christian fervor still remained (in American life), he was doubly so in observing that it had to be secularized before it could be exploited,' p. 463.
18. In analyzing a change in attitude of Americans toward gifts to Europe, Larrabee described the outlook of 'the American cynic' as illustrated by a Marshall Plan administrator who returned to Washington from Paris in 1952 to urge his superiors to invent a new set of motives to explain U.S. aid to Europeans. 'The more cold-blooded the better – to use in dealing with other nations,' the administrator urged. 'It would not matter whether they were true; they need only be credible, and they would be more credible to more people if they were based on a fairly selfish appreciation of the national self-interest.' See E. LARRABEE, 'Changing American Attitudes Toward Point IV,' p. 468. The actual preamble to the Economic Cooperation Agreement between the United States and France read in part: '... Recognizing that the restoration or maintenance ... of principles of individual liberty, free institutions and genuine independence rests largely upon sound economic conditions ... based upon a strong production effort, expansion of foreign trade, etc. ... the U.S. Government undertakes to assist France ...' (Source: *First Report to Congress of the Economic Cooperation Administration*, for the quarter ended June 30, 1948, pp. 58 ff.)
It is significant that 'self-interest' justifications for aid did not start until the early 1950's.

1960 when candidates argued over the respective standing of the United States and the Soviet Union in the eyes of Europeans, Asians, Africans, and others.[19] Some of the arguments were devoted to the relative ability of the United States and the Soviet Union to win friends and influence through foreign aid. Both adversaries, armed with nuclear weapons, competed with each other for world acceptance as the superior power, both claiming peace as the objective of gifts in the form of technical aid. The Marshall Plan was frequently invoked by the Americans as a plan of peaceful cooperation between free nations. These motives of gift-giving are strikingly close to such statements and ethnographic reports as Mauss made throughout his essay: a) 'Gifts to men and to gods have the . . . aim of buying peace';[20] b) referring to the Tlingit and Haida tribal practices of *potlatch* ceremonies, Mauss wrote: 'Essentially usurious and extravagant, it is above all a struggle among nobles to determine their position in the hierarchy to the ultimate benefit, if they are successful, of their own clans';[21] c) 'Between vassals and chiefs, between vassals and their henchmen, the hierarchy is established by means of . . . gifts,' Mauss said in interpreting the behavior of Trobriand and of Tsimshian chiefs;[22] and d) 'To give is to show one's superiority, to show that one is something more and higher, that one is *magister* . . . if one hoards, it is only to spend later on, to put people under obligation and to win followers.'[23]

The gift behavior of rival nations[24] of the contemporary world again comes to mind in connection with another analysis of gift practices by a student of pre-literate societies. Wardle wrote:

The voluntary offering of tangibles and intangibles designed to please or propitiate is a world-wide practice . . . Gifts serve both psychological and sociological ends, satisfying the ego through display and emulation, promoting friendship and solidarity of the group, maintaining wealth in a state of flux,

19. Among numerous press reports about prestige ratings during the months of October and November 1960, see for example, 'Post-Summit Trends in British and French Opinion on the United States and the Soviet Union,' Office of Research and Analysis, United States Information Agency, June 1960, reprinted in the *New York Times*, October 27, 1960, p. 28.
20. Mauss, *The Gift*, p. 14.
21. *Ibid.*, p. 4.
22. *Ibid.*, p. 72.
23. *Ibid.*, pp. 72-73.
24. An interesting development outside the familiar sphere of the U.S.-U.S.S.R. rivalry, illustrating further universality for Mauss' gift analysis, is the recent effort of the Arab League nations to compete with Israel by offering gifts (e.g., Arab cooperation in oil and commerce) to South Asians. See 'Arab League Sets Plan to Woo Asia,' *New York Times*, October 29, 1960, p. 3.

supporting religion and the primitive state, and *offering a substitute* [italics mine] for war and cementing alliances.[25]

Having suggested that the obligation to give can be traced to religious practices, the donor's desire to seek or maintain prestige, and the donor's search for peaceful relations with friendly followers, I wish now to refer briefly to the donor's expectation of returning gifts as a stimulus to making gifts.

3. *Expectation to Return Gifts*

The obligation to repay gifts, as it affects recipients, will be treated in Chapter IV. It cannot be entirely isolated, however, from the donor's obligation to give. Mauss was correct, I believe, in describing gift exchange as *total* phenomena,[26] a process of giving, receiving and repaying in which all the elements are thought to be 'at work' in every discrete act of the actors in the exchange. Thus the donor, at the moment of making a gift, is already being influenced by the expectation of a countergift even if the return a) may not be tendered in due season, until the next generation, or in the hereafter, or b) if the countergift may be of different value or kind.[27]

What return gifts did the United States expect from Europe in exchange for food, capital equipment, managerial and technical knowledge, and military protection? Some Americans would say nothing more than gratitude, a chance to do 'our Christian duty,' or, if it is a trait of American character to need to be loved, to be given respect and affection.[28] What-

25. See H. N. WARDLE, 'Gifts,' in *Encyclopedia of the Social Sciences* (New York: Macmillan & Co., 1931), Vol. III, pp. 657-658. Wardle's own research on gifts was published as an essay, 'Indian Gifts in Relation to Primitive Law,' in the International Congress of Americanists, *23rd Proceedings* (New York: 1930), pp. 463-469.
26. His discussion of *total presentations* or 'wholes' is relevant here. See M. MAUSS, *The Gift*, pp. 3 and 76-77.
27. The philosophical and economic questions of 'value' are beyond this study, though inevitably related to an analysis of gifts. Mauss' own interests in markets, barter, currency, and calculations of property value, however, are found throughout his essay. The political economy of gifts as objects of value would include both Keynsian and Marxist theory, and such historical and anthropological perspectives as are found in K. POLANYI, C. M. ARENSBERG and H. W. PEARSON, *Trade and Markets in the Early Empires* (Glencoe, Ill., Free Press, 1957).
28. Eric Larrabee has amplified this point in a essay already quoted: 'Point IV ... has served as a focus for the shifting public apprehensions of the problems and obligations that "development" implies ... Some (educationists, internationalists, journalists) wanted to be sure that their sympathies were not being exploited.' See 'Changing American Attitudes ... ,' p. 456. They were skeptical, Larrabee wrote, because they wanted to be convinced that foreign aid was not 'a veiled device to make profits abroad for American business.' They believed that 'the less fortunate parts of the world ought to be "civilized" ... into approximate facsimiles of America.' (*Ibid.*, p. 457.) This suggests that a proper 'return gift' might be evidence

ever the expectation, the aid offered had the effect of permitting American troops to be based on European soil, in quarters mainly financed by Americans, and of encouraging some Americans to think that anti-Communist voting would be *quid pro quo*. The field work I have done in France strongly points to the conclusion that, from a French recipient's point of view, such countergifts failed to match French notions of proper repayment. Nevertheless, the American donor, like the chiefs and noble hosts among the primitives and ancients, offered gifts with an expectation of return of some kind. The Marshall Plan was regarded by one European intellectual as 'a superb piece of statesmanship, one of the highlights of the history of mankind. . .'[29] Such recognition of generosity, however, did not exempt American donors from what Mauss called the subject matter of his essay: 'In theory . . . gifts are voluntary, but in fact they are given and repaid under obligation.'[30]

B. THE SOCIAL ARRANGEMENTS AROUND GIFTS

The preceding section represents an effort to find a rough classification of motives which have inspired men in general, and Americans in particular, to offer gifts both within and outside their social groups or nations. This section will represent a search for an answer to the related question: What can the offering of a gift tell us about the rank of the donor or the social relationships within which gifts are given?

A more thorough search for an answer to this question would require an analysis of a) gifts in hierarchies, i.e., downward and upward giving (tribute); b) gifts between equals;[31] and c) the distinction between gift

that the recipient liked the donor well enough to pattern his values and behavior after him.

29. SALVADOR DE MADARIAGA, 'Why Americans are Unpopular,' *World Liberalism*, Vol. 7, No. 2 (Summer 1957), p. 16.

30. M. MAUSS, *The Gift*, p. 1.

31. For example, gifts exchanged between two heads of state, lieutenants in the same infantry company, chiefs of two neighbouring tribes, siblings in the same family, or nurses in the same hospital ward. Such relationships reflect the actors' *equivalent* positions in formal social structures. See discussions of equivalence in ELIOT CHAPPLE and CARLETON COON, *Principles of Anthropology* (New York: Henry Holt, 1942), especially the analysis of Riffian family organization in which first cousins occupy similar positions to those of a brother and sister in a unit family, p. 306. Another reference to sibling equivalences is in ROBERT LOWIE, *Social Organization* (New York: Rinehard, 1948), p. 94. These examples do not take into account differences of sex or age which also may have a bearing on donor-recipient relationships, that is, where male dominance or age difference operate.

behavior and market behavior.[32] Because U.S. technical assistance to France represented giving from a stronger, bigger, richer nation to a weaker, smaller, older nation, I shall concentrate here on the type of social arrangements in which the donor occupies a dominant or superordinate position vis-à-vis the recipient.

Mauss wrote about gift exchange and the social position of the donor before such concepts as 'status-building,' 'status-maintaining,' or 'status deprivation' entered the vocabulary of social scientist and their readers. However, it is clear from Mauss' discussion of the obligation to give that he regarded hierarchical relationship as characteristic of much of the gift-giving which he studied. In a statement quoted at the beginning of this chapter, Mauss wrote that gifts (food, women, labor, charms, etc.) pass and repass 'between clans and individuals, *ranks*, sexes and generations.'[33] For Mauss, the most conspicuous example of gifts being offered by 'superiors' to 'inferiors,' from those of upper ranks to those of lower ranks, was the potlatch institution. The Chinook Indian word, potlatch, referring to the unique institutionalized gift behavior of Northwest Coast Indians, was used by Mauss in a more general sense to describe cycles of giving and taking, or interaction between donors and recipients, in various parts of the world. The main social trait is that the host or donor *initiates* a gift

---

32. Mauss' interest in various forms of contract and exchange led him to questioning differences between gift exchange and market transactions. 'It has been suggested that these (archaic) societies lack the economic market, but this is not true; for the market is a human phenomenon which we believe to be familiar in every known society. Markets are found before the development of merchants . . . and currency as we know it.' (*The Gift*, p. 2.) In the meantime, a sharper distinction has been provided by Conrad M. Arensberg: 'We find that gift-giving does the same things for individual and social life as does the market. Both are mechanisms of distribution and survival. But they are different mechanisms, based on very different social arrangements, in many ways opposite cultural and institutional elaborations.' (See his chapter 'Anthropology as History,' in *Trade and Markets in the Early Empires*, p. 112.) These observations could stimulate cross-cultural comparisons of how people in different societies rank buyers and sellers in their transactions, e.g., notions of merchant inferiority in classical China, the American adage that 'the customer is always right,' and, according to my observations, the contempt French *vendeurs* hold for their customers, who seem to represent intrusions on the sellers' property and privacy.

33. *The Gift*, p. 12. See also FRANZ BOAZ, *Contribution to the Ethnology of the Kwakiutl* (New York: Columbia University Press, 1925), for a fine record of blanket and dance giving involving ranks, pp. 135-145 and PHILIP DRUCKER and ROBERT F. HEIZER, *To Make My Good: A Reexamination of The Southern Kwakiutl Potlatch*, Berkeley and Los Angeles, University of California Press, 1967. An African perspective on gifts and solidarity can be found in *Farnham* REHFISCH, 'Competitive Gift Exchange among The Nambila,' *Cahiers d'Etudes Africaines*, Vol. III, No. 9, 1962.

(feast) as an expression of his rank.[34] He may invite and give in order to build up his rank in the eyes of others who previously invited him. Or he may give a potlatch (ceremony) in order to maintain his position in a hierarchy whether or not he is under an obligation. Hierarchy is established or maintained by means of gifts. To give is to show one's superiority.

Prestige, rank, or top place in an international hierarchy may now be the preoccupation of some Americans. Such national goals, however, were not self-consciously sought at the end of World War II when the United States reluctantly took on 'great power' status with its incumbent obligation to give, to teach, or to heal.[35] The administrators of American aid had no potlatch-like intentions to wound others with charity or to humiliate recipients with gifts. Only in conflict with the Russians did Americans enter into situations in which, reminiscent of the Kwakiutl and Haida noblemen, the *persona* ('face' and status) was at stake and threatened with loss if lesser peoples failed to receive from them, as gifts, the industrial equivalents of 'the produce of the chase or the forest which the gods or totems have sent'.[36] It is from the perspective of the recipient (to be dis-

34. A more ambitious study of gift exchange than this one would make use of the growing literature on theoretical and empirical studies of human interaction, the situation in which the actions of one individual are followed by the actions of another. (See CHAPPLE *et al.*, *Principles of Anthropology*, p. 705.) The man who *initiates action*, i.e. offers gifts, provides clues to a study of social structure and social action. Arensberg, for example, wrote: 'Where determining the order of action or initiative between persons is part of the observation which goes into discriminations of status and relationships, that operation must also carry over into our models of institution, social arrangement, economic system, etc.' (See his essay in *Trade and Market in the Early Empires*, p. 98.) Thus, if a chief, or head of an industrial nation, offers gifts, he is initiating a donor-recipient relationship *if* the gifts are accepted. The originator of the gift then takes on a position, if not already established by other means, of being a leader, or in authority and exercising social control over the recipient. (Cf. Correspondence from George Homans to William F. Whyte quoted in Whyte's mimeographed draft of a research review for *Human Organization* entitled: 'Interaction: Method and Theory,' No. 58-1219, p. 19.) Mauss wrote: 'The obligation to give is the essence of the *potlatch* ... The chief must give a potlatch ... keep authority ... maintain position. Failing these obligations – at least for the nobles – etiquette is violated and rank is lost.' (See *The Gift*, pp. 37-38.)
35. Max Lerner, in his chapter 'America as a World Power', in *America as a Civilization* (New York: Simon and Schuster, 1957), pp. 879-950, traces both American and other ambivalence toward the superior power and responsibility of the United States after the World War II. For other discussions of the growth of the idea of public service and world responsibility as characteristic of the American 'self-image', see also: DAVID M. POTTER, *People of Plenty* (Chicago: University of Chicago Press, 1954), and JOHN K. GALBRAITH, *The Affluent Society* (Boston: Houghton Mifflin Co., 1958).
36. *The Gift*, p. 38.

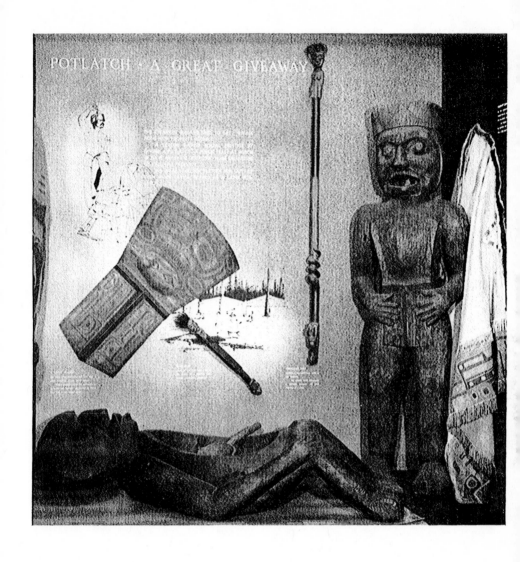

Examples of gifts used by the leaders of the Kwakiutl Indians at a potlach – a feast where they gave away huge quantities of valuable property to show their superiority.

cussed in Chapter III) that American gifts were mainly seen as an expression of rank, as a threat to the rank of the recipient, or as a sign of the superiority of the donor.

A helpful comparative view of the American donor-teacher position vis-à-vis France is to be found in Natalie Joffe's analysis of benefice among East European Jews. While her observations referred only to ingroup behavior, her generalizations are applicable to understanding Americans' donor relationships with the French. She wrote:

> For a society within the Western cultural tradition, East European Jewish culture exhibits a minimum of reciprocal behavior. Wealth, learning and other tangible and intangible possessions are fluid and are channeled so that in the main they flow from the 'strong', or 'rich', or 'learned', or 'older', to those who are 'weaker', 'poorer', 'ignorant', or 'younger'. Therefore all *giving* is downward . . . It is mandatory for the good things of life to be shared or passed downward during one's lifetime . . . The concept of the good deed, the *Mitzvah*, is not voluntary – it has been enjoined upon every Jew by God . . . It is shameful . . . to receive succor of any sort from those who are inferior to you in status. To receive any (return gifts) implies that you are in a position to be controlled, for the reciprocal of the downward giving is deference.[37]

The Marshall Plan represented a similar phenomenon on a larger scale. Downward giving was its *leitmotif*. The 'good things of life' (machines, capital, knowledge of industrial and agricultural productivity, better 'human relations in industry', etc.) were to be shared and passed down to people who were weaker, poorer, and less learned in the ways of industrial civilization. The main contrasting elements were: a) Americans, as aid administrators, gave to members of an out-group rather than, as did the East European Jews, to members of their own community, and b) Americans, from the standpoint of age-grading among nations, were giving as age juniors to age seniors, and expected gratitude more than deference in return. From interview responses of American administrators of aid, I assume that France, pictured often as 'the tired, old man,' was perceived by Americans in the same light as the aged in the United States. That is, both public and family funds are needed to take care of elders at the hand of the stronger, younger persons who, whether new or old Americans, are trained to be independent in the wisdom and rule of the elders and are thought to be more efficient in the way of the modern world.[38]

37. NATALIE F. JOFFE, 'Non-Reciprocity among East European Jews,' in MARGARET MEAD and RHODA MÉTRAUX, eds., *The Study of Culture at a Distance* (Chicago: University of Chicago Press, 1953), p. 386-387. Symmetrical behavior, the give and take between equals, is illustrated here by the exchange of *Schalochmones* (sweetmeats) by women at Purim time and two men taking care of each other during illness.

38. A convenient summary of the literature on age-grading within specific societies

Parallel patterns of dominance and submission, and giving and receiving, then, were the main characteristics of American-French relationships during the Marshall Plan. American gifts were offered, not through carefully prescribed and understood social institutions (e.g., *potlatch* or *kula*), but through social arrangements which, though fluid and uninstitutionalized, bore striking similarities to Mauss' analysis of societies where rank, superior strength, wealth, and religion were incorporated into the donor's obligation to give.

C. KNOWLEDGE AS GIFT: THE TRANSFER OF 'KNOW-HOW'

Having already inferred that the possession of superior knowledge – cosmological, technical, or sacred[39] – may influence the ranking of a

---

is the discussion of age status in KINGSLEY DAVIS, *Human Society* (New York: Macmillan Company, 1950), pp. 103-110. To my knowledge, there is no study yet made of international age-grading, i.e., the projections of national or societal age rankings on the international scene as a factor in the social arrangements of foreign aid. The young nations of Africa have both power and prestige within the United Nations context, but are recipients of bi-lateral aid from the older, richer nations. Part of the jockeying for self-esteem on the part of the young, African recipients of aid is manifest in the Africans' search for a golden, pre-European age, preferably an epoch of tribal glory when Europeans were young savages and Africans were in an advanced stage of bronze sculpture and political organization. Another source of self-esteem, at least for one African intellectual with whom I talked in Sierra Leone in 1960, is to remember that African societies were donors, though unwilling, of valuable human gifts (slaves) who thereby put Western nations under an obligation to pay back new African nations with capital and technical assistance today. 'If you should create a Marshall Plan for Africa,' he said, 'we would consider this reciprocation for our past contributions to the building of your economy and civilization.' Thus the age of a nation as a political entity may be an independent variable in analyzing how nations 'keep records' of their felt obligations.

39. Assuming that common-sense and scientific knowledge represent techniques by which man is able to adjust himself to the basic kinds of terrestrial environment making up the earth's surface (boreal, mountain, polar and scrub forest lands, grasslands, etc.), and that cosmological and sacred knowledge helps man to control and interpret his universe, we are in a position to escape Alfred North Whitehead's injunction: '... The notion of "more knowledge" is a high abstraction which we should dismiss from our minds.' See *Adventure of Ideas* (New York: Mentor, 1955), p. 12. See also Kroeber's discussion of the functional connection between object and idea in his distinction between material and non-material culture. In A. L. KROEBER, *Anthropology* (New York: Harcourt, Brace & Co., 1948), he wrote: 'What counts is not the physical ax or coat but the idea of them, the knowledge how to produce and use them, their place in life. It is this knowledge, concept and function that get themselves handed down through the generations, or diffused into other cultures, while the objects themselves are quickly worn out or consumed.' (P. 295.) Also

nation in international hierarchies, and thus become part of the 'stuff that is given away and repaid,'[40] I now wish to conclude this chapter with an affirmative answer to the question: Can knowledge, considered as a gift, become part of a nation's obligation to give? Knowledge, like the beads, pottery, or food which circulates in exchanges between people in simple societies, is a commodity of considerable value in highly specialized, industrial nations. The obligation to give knowledge from a technologically advanced nation to a technologically backward nation may not have the same motive force as the religious fervor which drove Islamic or Christian missionaries to other lands. However, in an increasingly industrialized and urbanized world, knowledge of machines and the techniques of organizing and managing work is in short supply.[41] Those nations which possess such knowledge are under obligation, from within and without, to transfer 'know-how' to those who lack it.[42] Giving is generally downward, going from the teacher-donor to the pupil-recipient, with international technical assistance serving as a classroom writ large.

The case study of Monsieur B. in the next chapter will give empirical support to the point that the giving of both tangibles (machines, money, food) and intangibles (knowledge about organizing work) from Americans to Frenchmen was perceived by the recipients as downward giving. Having concentrated in this chapter on the ethos and obligations of donors, whether tribal or national, I wish to add a closing statement about Americans as international donors and teachers. Margaret Mead wrote:

Our ambivalence, as Americans, about the role of the federal government, at home and abroad, is a compound of our dislike of the federal government's getting into habits of playing Santa Claus and *our dislike of anyone receiving hand-outs* [italics mine]. The genius of the Point Four program was that it emphasized the role of Americans, acting through the federal government, in *providing 'know-how' rather than goods* [italics mine], in helping other people to help themselves . . .[43]

The social arrangement of offering and distributing gifts of knowledge to

---

pertinent here is FLORIN ZNANIECKI, *The Social Role of the Man of Knowledge* (New York: Columbia University Press, 1940), esp. Ch. II, 'Technologists and Sages,' pp. 23-90.

40. *The Gift*, p. 12.
41. See PEARL FRANKLIN CLARK in *The Challenge of American Know-How* (New York: Harper & Co., 1948), p. 172, and MARY CUSHING NILES, *The Essence of Management* (New York: Harper & Co., 1958), esp. pp. 36-37.
42. See the editorial, 'International Exchange of Know-How,' in *Modern Industry*, October 15, 1951, p. 176.
43. See her essay, 'Christian Faith and Technical Assistance', in WAYNE H. COWAN, ed., *What the Christians hopes for in Society* (New York: Association Press, 1957), p. 90.

B., as we shall see, were of a bilateral nature, highlighting the cultural contrasts in French and American perceptions of the offering of 'know-how.'[44]

44. Of such bilateral giving, Mead also wrote: 'In giving technical assistance today and helping other peoples to overcome starvation, ignorance or preventable disease, we have the choice of acting bilaterally, as members of a single, very rich, very prosperous, generous, but necessarily self-interested (for it is the function of national governments to protect their own people against all others) nation-state, or as members of an associated group of nations, in which we who wish to help and they who need help meet in an equality of interest and dignity ... Simple sharing, not lordly benefaction, enobles both giver and receiver while the least extra, unnecessary, in a sense technological discrepancy, begrimes and demeans such sharing.' ('Christian Faith and Technical Assistance,' p. 91.)

CHAPTER III

THE OBLIGATION TO RECEIVE

A. THE CASE OF MONSIEUR B.: A STUDY IN AMBIVALENCE

The obligation to receive, Mauss wrote, is no less constraining than the obligation to give. 'One does not have the right to refuse a gift or a potlatch.'[1] Referring to such exceptions as high-ranking Kwakiutls who were so securely recognized in the hierarchy that they could refuse without a war ensuing, Mauss then made generalizations about the sanctions which move people to accept gifts. For example:

You accept (e.g., the food of Kwakiutls) and you do so because you mean to take up the challenge and prove that you are not unworthy . . . *Failure to give or receive, like failure to make return gifts, means a loss of dignity* . . .[2] To refuse to give, or to fail to invite, is – like refusing to accept – the equivalent of a declaration of war; it is a refusal of friendship and intercourse.[3]

Extending Mauss' generalizations to organized technical assistance between industrial nations, I am suggesting not that war follows when nations refuse gifts but that the recipient's need (for economic improvement, knowledge, etc.) and desires for friendly relations oblige nations to accept. Gift-avoidance or gift-rejection could be considered unfriendly in the eyes of the initiator of gifts.[4] Nations, like individuals, families or tribes, must reconcile

1. MAUSS, *The Gift*, p. 39.
2. *Ibid.*, p. 40.
3. *Ibid.*, p. 11.
4. Burma's experience with rejecting aid, or placing conditions on the donor if aid was to be accepted, would be a fruitful subject of further study. Both the United States and the U.S.S.R., as donor nations, have encountered 'difficulties' in inducing the Burmese to recognize the obligation to receive. Burma terminated Point Four aid and later, before accepting a fully-staffed hospital as a Soviet gift, insisted on making return gift of rice which the Soviets did not want. John Montgomery, Boston University, will treat some aspects of the Burma case in his forthcoming book, *The Politics of Foreign Aid in South Asia*, to be published for the Council on Foreign Relations.

desires for friendly relations with gift-offering donors, on one hand, and desires for autonomy, independence, and freedom from obligation, on the other. The psychological concept of *ambivalence* – the co-existence of opposite and conflicting feelings about the same person or subject – is useful in understanding the types of obligation at work in technical assistance.

To illustrate both the obligation to receive and, in the next chapter, the obligation to repay, I will now introduce a case study of Monsieur B., a French engineer and small factory owner, who acted on his obligation to receive gifts from the United States in the form of technical and managerial knowledge. His case represents the twin themes of a) accepting American gifts for their utilitarian value (i.e., the improvement of living standards to help himself, his family, and the nation), and b) the quest for ways to maintain personal and national honor and dignity while being a recipient and pupil, i.e., the object of downward giving of goods and instruction. This is a study of ambivalence: it describes the desire of a man to accept what is offered, while at the same time deprecating the value of the gifts and the motives of the donor, in order to maintain self-respect and to reduce the weight of the obligation.

Remembering Mauss' statement that the study of the concrete is the study of 'the whole,' in presenting this case I shall be moving back and forth between different levels of analysis: the individual, the family, the world of work and peers, the nation, and the alliance of which the nation is a part. It is through these networks of relationships that I will examine the distribution of knowledge, perceived as a gift, and what happens to the gift in the process, as well as the relationships between the donor and the recipient. The individual, as a recipient of gifts who wants to make return gifts, will be seen as a personality representing an organization of these many interrelations into a whole.[5]

5. The rationale for using a single case as a unit of analysis (to illustrate the dynamics of the Marshall Plan as a system of gift exchange) is based in part on the following assumption: The exchange between individuals of different nations can constitute the gift behavior of nations if the self is identified with the national symbols or goals. In his *Criteria for the Life History* (New Haven: Yale University Press, 1935) John Dollard argues for studies of individual behavior: 'In the long-section or life history view the individual remains organically present as an object of study; he must be accounted for in his full, immediate, personal reality. The eye remains on the details of his behavior and these we must research on, and explain. Here culture is bedded down in a specific organic locus. The culture forms a continuous and connected wrap for the organic life ... The person is viewed as an organic center of feeling moving through a culture and drawing magnetically to him the main strands of the culture. *In the end the individual appears as a person, as a microcosm of the group features of his culture* [italics mine]. It is possible that detailed studies of the lives of individuals will reveal new perspectives on the culture as a whole which are not accessible when one remains on the formal cross-sectional

Before B. left to accept American offers of 'know-how',[6] he had learned

plans of observation.' (p. 4.) Robert Redfield, in *The Little Community: Viewpoints for the Study of a Human Whole* (Chicago: University of Chicago Press, 1955), stated: 'Humanity presents itself to the view of common sense in just a few kinds of integral entities. A person is one such kind of entity, a separate and unique human individual ... Yet another, characteristic of our times but not of all, is the national state. A fourth, more difficult to delimit and to characterize even than these others, is a civilization. Person, people, nation, and civilization are forms of humanity, each kind of which constitutes a great and easily recognizable class, and each separate one of which is describable in its own characteristics as a whole (p. 1). Each person, each stable human settlement with an organized way of life, each historical people, even each art or body of literature associated with such a people, has a sort of integrity which is recognized by common sense and by much scholarship, humanistic and anthropological.' (p. 2.)

Through her studies of culture and personality, Margaret Mead draws attention to the process by which individuals learn reciprocal and other types of behavior. For example, in *Male and Female* (New York: William Morrow & Co., 1949), Mead discusses the patterning of reciprocal relationships, locating the pattern in the 'behavior of the mother and child ... as involving an interchange when the child takes in what the mother gives it, and later, in elimination, makes a return.' This represents 'an exchange of commodities between mother and child. Such behavior can be called *reciprocal*. In reciprocal phrasings of relationship, love, trust, tears, may become commodities, just as much as physical objects, but the interchange of physical objects remains the prototype.' (pp. 64-65.)

Such childhood training of individuals, leading to the varying degrees to which cultures may emphasize reciprocity (as compared with symmetrical or complementary behavior), has been hypothesized by Gregory Bateson in 'Formulation of End Linkage,' in MARGARET MEAD and RHODA MÉTRAUX, *op. cit.*, pp. 367-378. This essay also appears as 'Morale and National Character' in G. WATSON, ed., *Civilian Morale* (Boston: Houghton Mifflin, 1942), pp. 71-91. He suggests how adult behavior is molded and that such behavior may show a certain consistency in various institutions making up a national culture (e.g., family, religion, politics, etc.).

In their study of Japanese students and scholars, *In Search of Identity* (Minneapolis: University of Minnesota Press, 1958), John W. Bennett, Herbert Passin, and Robert K. McKnight devote some attention to relationships between the self and the nation as a problem in identity. Borrowing, no doubt, from George H. Mead's *Mind, Self and Society* (Chicago: University of Chicago Press, 1934), their comments on the Japanese provide a strong reminder of the case of Monsieur B.: 'Educated Japanese with a sense of pride in the work of transformation, or through personal identification equate with the prestige of the nation while travelling abroad, have tended to national and personal identity. Indeed, it is our conviction that this tendency to equate the nation and the individual in search for identity is widespread and forms a major problem of intercultural relations in the modern world.' (p. 8.) 'The search for identity is ... for many Japanese, tantamount to a search for the self.' (p. 25.)

6. The administrative and political background of U.S. aid programs related to France is outside the scope of this study. The details of the aid program, however, from both American and French sources, can be found in HARRY BAYARD PRICE, *The Meaning of the Marshall Plan* (Ithaca: Cornell University Press, 1955);

an elaborate set of implicit rules about giving gifts, receiving gifts, and repaying obligations. He learned these first in the contexts of his family and church and then these rules became a part of his conduct of business and profession during adult life. (See diagram.) His life history shows a consistent pattern of giving and receiving. As a boss (*patron*) and head of family, he was more often the donor than the receiver in a variety of ceremonial and work situations in France. As chief of an industrial mission to the U.S., he reversed his role and what he perceived to be the historical, national role of France. The self and the nation were more accustomed to giving and teaching than to receiving and learning. He accepted the temporary role reversal in travelling to the U.S. because he wanted France to catch up with the rest of the world in fields of technical knowledge which the nation had missed as a result of war.[7] He accepted what he thought would be a temporary decline in personal and national prestige (i.e., becoming dependent on people perceived as 'too young' and 'culturally inferior') with the expectation that he as an individual and France as a nation would become stronger (i.e., restore *grandeur*) and be able to return the favor.[8]

JEAN-ROGER HERRENSCHMIDT, *Problems of Technical Assistance:* The Experience of the Economic Cooperation, Administration and the Mutual Security Agency in France. (Unpublished Ph.D. dissertation, Harvard University, 1954); HENRY W. EHR-MANN, *Organized Business in France* (Princeton: Princeton University Press, 1957); and *Actions et Problèmes de Productivité*, First Report of the National Productivity Committee, Paris, 1953.

7. Such travel was not new in world history. In relations between pre-industrial civilizations, knowledge also was an objective of travel across cultural frontiers. Guy S. Métraux, in a historical view of cross-cultural education, wrote: 'If a society becomes conscious of the need for knowledge, skills or techniques that it does not possess, one way to acquire them is by resorting to temporary emigration to such areas as do possess them. Since it cannot migrate *in corpore* it is easier to encourage selected members of the group to go out to other groups where such knowledge is available and bring it back.' (See 'Cross-Cultural Education through the Ages,' reprinted in *International Education: A Documentary History*, Teachers College Classics in Education, No. 5, Columbia University, New York, 1960, p. 125, originally in *International Social Science Bulletin*, Vol. VIII, No. 4, Paris, UNESCO, 1956, pp. 577-584.) Knowledge of Buddhism was the object of travel for hundreds of Asians coming to the University of Nalanda, India, between the 5th and 12th centuries, A.D. Similarly, China and Rome were places to which people travelled to seek the gifts of enlightenment, power, or status associated with centers of imperial power. (Cf. DAVID G. MANDELBAUM, 'Comments,' *Journal of Social Issues*, Vol. 12, pp. 45-46.)

8. For an interesting comparison of how family relationships can shape perceptions of international affairs in another society, see RUTH BUNZEL and JOHN H. WEAKLAND, 'An Anthropological Approach to Chinese Communism,' *Columbia University Research in Contemporary Cultures*, 1952 (dittoed). An excerpt of the paper appears

NETWORKS IN EXCHANGE RELATIONSHIPS IN WHICH MONSIEUR B. PARTICI-
PATED BEFORE VOYAGE TO THE UNITED STATES IN 1952

*(Diagram identifies various contexts through which B. learned reciprocal
behavior and which influenced his expectations of exchange relationships
vis-à-vis Americans.)*

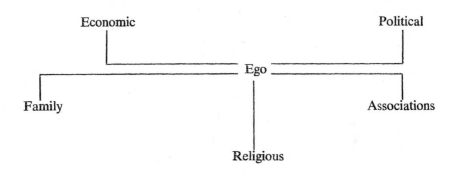

1. *Family:*   Gives protection, money, food, shelter, love, etc.
                  Receives love, emotional support, prestige, etc.
2. *Economic:*   Gives, to workers, money, protection, security.
                  Receives work in form of finished goods to sell.
3. *Religious:*   Gives prayers, money, family, etc.
                  Receives protection, security, rationale for life.
4. *Political:*   Gives time and vote to General de Gaulle.
                  Receives identity, protection, direction, self-esteem.
5. *Associations:* Give time, money, service.
                  Receive recognition, pleasure of belonging, sense of
                  autonomy by choosing associations and being 'goal-
                  directed.'

---

as 'Chinese Family Images in International Affairs' in MARGARET MEAD and RHODA
MÉTRAUX, *op. cit.*, pp. 421-426. Remembering that my informant sometimes referred
to the French as the 'Chinese of Europe' (reflecting the 18th century French ration-
alists' admiration for Chinese ethics and family-oriented statecraft), I have been
struck by the following account of the way Chinese see reciprocity: 'For Chinese,
"inequality" appears to involve particularly a fear that the occupant of the position
of superior power will use that power to take advantage of the occupant of a
weaker position, especially to make demands on the services or resources of the
weaker *without making a reciprocal return*. Such a fear appears not only in regard
to relations between nations ... but also ... individuals.' *Ibid.*, p. 424. Both the
Chinese and the French seem to fear one-sided relationships, preferring those that
are mutually advantageous. Prototypes for such feelings may be found in traditional
extended family relationships.

How does B.'s life history reflect some of the social and cultural sources of his ambivalent feeling toward the United States as a donor and himself and France as recipients?

Born in 1898 as the first child of Paul and Madeleine B., he spent his early childhood in Paris and in the Lorraine village which I will call Vincent. In this village, several generations of the B. family are buried. The father was also an engineer, attaining the rank in the French civil service as inspector general of bridges and roads. Whether in Paris or in Vincent, the B. family devotedly followed the liturgical cycle of the Roman Catholic Church. As a boy, B. memorised the Saints' Days of his relatives, and as an adult he required his own children to do the same and to remember these relatives with gifts. Similarly, they expected to be remembered with gifts by relatives and friends on their own Saints' Days. The gifts were rarely of great intrinsic value, being candy or flowers. Special foods were prepared for the person being honored.

On the road to Vincent, the town of Notre Dame d'Epinay is noted for its manufacture of candy-coated almonds (*dragées*). The present B. family stops there regularly to purchase supplies of these sweets. They are typical gifts for presentation at baptisms and first communions. B. says that he averages at least a dozen such ceremonies a year for children of relatives or friends. The friends who are identified with the family through military service or wartime resistance work are considered closer than other friends, and special attention is given to remembering their children and accepting invitations related to their *rites de passage*.

The obligation felt by B. to give both gifts and his presence at such ceremonies is strong enough so that he has interrupted a family vacation to return to Paris for the baptism of a niece, or he has left his factory during the demands of filling work orders to drive more than a hundred miles to be present for a first communion in the country. Kinship and friendship ties, the latter reinforced by shared war experiences, are manifest in the religious ceremonies which mark the various stages of the life cycle. Gifts are part of the interaction process.[9]

9. I have made observations of similar practices among members of the aristocracy in Lorraine, Brittany, and Provence.

The circulation of gifts follows the same pattern, moreover, among peers of the B. family in Paris, members of the industrial and professional bourgeoisie. For a brief portrait of the ethos of bourgeois families, see John B. Christopher, 'The Dessication of the Bourgeois Spirit,' in E. M. EARLE, ed., *Modern France* (Princeton University Press, 1951), pp. 44-57; and JULIAN PITT-RIVERS, *Social Class in a French Village* (dittoed, 1958), p. 8. Pitt-Rivers, incidentally, finds that the elites in France provide the common factors in French culture, and that the peasants account for the

Mauss, who himself grew up in Lorraine, gave the following description of gift obligations and practices in France in the late nineteenth century:

Our morality is not solely commercial. We still have people and classes who uphold past customs and we bow to them on special occasions and at certain periods of the year . . . Just as a courtesy has to be returned, so must an invitation. Here we find traces of the traditional basis, the aristocratic potlatch; and we see at work also some of the fundamental motives of human activity: emulation between individuals of the same sex, the basic 'imperialism' of men – of origin part social, part animal or psychological no doubt . . . A family of my childhood in Lorraine . . . would face ruin for the sake of its guests on Saints' Days, weddings, first communions and funerals. You had to be a *grand seigneur* on these occasions. Some of our people behave like this all the time and spend money recklessly on their guests, parties and New Year gifts. Invitations have to be offered and have to be accepted.[10]

A more recent French observer of ceremonial gift practices in rural France also describes baptism such as Monsieur B. often attends. In their study of Nouville, Bernot and Blancard report:

On the day of the ceremony, the woman who has helped the mother during her confinement carries the infant to the church . . . One offers blue or pink candied almonds (*dragées*) the sex of the infant, a custom which did not exist before the war of 1914 when one offered white *dragées* or mixed ones. Let us notice that if the child belongs to a worker's family, the boss (*patron*) pays for a part of the *dragées*.[11]

The above vignette of gift behavior in France introduces other aspects of B.'s exchange relationships which led him to expect certain responses from Americans when he travelled to the United States. In his role as head of a Roman Catholic family, B., as we have just seen, acts as a donor in a variety of religious and *rites de passage* situations involving kin and non-kin. How do these habits appear in his role as *patron* in the factory? The baptism described above is marked by a *patron* paying for part of the *dragées* offered to the infant of a worker. B. makes no sharp distinction in his own mind between his role as head of family and as head of factory. In an interview in September 1956, he said:

I am the one who has to pay. Whether one likes it or not, one must give *cadeaux* (gifts). And yet there will always be people who will envy. One must

---

regional diversity in France. (See *Conference on French Community Studies*, Haverford College, September 9-12, 1956.)

10. *The Gift*, pp. 63-64.
11. See Lucien Bernot and René Blancard, *Nouville, un village français* (Paris: Travaux et Mémoires de l'Institut d'Ethnologie – LVII, 1952), p. 112.

prepare oneself to be the crystallization of external forces, and to take the blows (*coups*) which come to those in authority.

From his children, two daughters and a son, B. does not expect blows, either physical or verbal. He is the protector, provider, and disciplinarian, rewarding the children with gifts and verbal praise, or reproaching them, as their comportment or school marks may require. However, he is aware that he is the restraining influence and must not always expect complete adherence to his wishes. Some grumbling, so long as it is not openly disrespectful, is expected from both his children and workers. ('Frenchmen are individualists.') The *patron* in France has had to learn to live in a somewhat hostile environment. Gifts and other rewards are among the instruments for trying to deal with such an environment.

In December 1952, shortly before his departure for the United States, he detected plans at his factory for a walk-out strike. His foreman had overheard some workers discussing such plans and reported the plans to B. This was the *patron's* cue to offer a more elaborate New Year's party than he had planned and to advance the date of it before Christmas to allow him a cermonial chance to distribute the usual end-of-year bonuses. The timing of the party, and the slight increase in the size of the bonuses, forestalled the strike. During the same week, B. distributed money to the doorman, postman, and ice deliveryman in his Neuilly apartment house.

In June 1956, an Arab worker at B.'s factory asked the *patron* for permission to leave work for two days to attend to problems of burying a brother, Ahmed, who had died of a heart attack while off-duty from his work at the SIMCA automobile factory. B. responded by offering to pay for the burial, by arranging to have an Arabic-speaking French *officier des affaires indigènes* (an ex-colonial officer) notify the kinsmen in Algeria, and by hiring an *imam* (Moslem prayer leader) to conduct the services. On July 16, 1956, the end of Bastille Day demonstrations by Algerians at the Place de la République, B. summoned Kazam and asked: 'If your comrades tell you to go on strike during the vacation, when you are alone guarding the factory, what will you do, Kazam?' The *patron* told him that he was aware he would run the risk of being knifed (*coup de couteau*) by other Algerian members of an Islamic fraternal organization who were organizing sympathy strikes to protest French resistance against Algerian rebellion. Kazam told B. that he would not leave the plant unprotected, that he would guard it despite the pressures of other Algerians to make him join the strikes. The *patron*, in describing this understanding with Kazam, his oldest Algerian worker, said:

We depend on each other. He has worked for me almost 12 years. Without him I could not count on the work of the other Algerians. He is top man and being the oldest, I depend on him to control the others . . . Kazam knows that he can depend on me when he is in trouble.

Thus we can see the web of obligation binding B.'s relationship with friends, kinsmen, and workers. Gifts take the form of money and services. In the worlds of family and factory, he is involved in chains of giving and receiving.[12] When the chains appear to be breaking (e.g., the threatened strike at the factory), B. offers gifts and a temporary balance is established by this.

In other situations, where there appear to be no strains, gifts are offered to prevent strains or to provide assurances that he desires the relationship to continue. In July 1956, B., for example, staged an elaborate ceremonial party to celebrate the completion of repairs on the small family chateau in the Lorraine village of Vincent. The party was offered as a gift to the whole village to announce that the B. family was once again taking up its 'seat' there. (The chateau had been badly damaged by artillery fire during World War II.) The workers were special guests of honor. As they were related to almost every family in the village, the attention given to them for their work was, by extension, a recognition of the whole village. A neighboring nobleman, François de C., was invited to cut the ribbon to commemorate the completion of repairs. From the villagers, the B. family received respect and recognition and services related to the small farm and the cutting and planting of trees in the forest. In exchange, the B. family offered some wages, but, above all, the villagers had the distinction of having the most imposing structure in the village occupied by a family that represented (a) continuity (the B. family crypt near the village chapel contained several generations), and (b) sacrifice (Monsieur B., as an officer in both World Wars, had personally defended the village with artillery; and his sister, Denise, died in a concentration camp for her resistance

12. Cf. WILTON S. DILLON, 'Allah Loves Strong Men,' *Columbia University Forum*, Vol. IV, No. 1 (Winter 1961), pp. 45-47. A more detailed treatment of B.'s relations with his children and his workers is found in an unpublished paper, Dillon, W., 'Islam and Authority Patterns in a French Factory: The Role of Kinship and Religion in Boss-Worker Relationships' (Typescript, 1956), p. 55. The following excerpt from it suggests the similarity to be found between B.'s behavior at home and at the factory: 'Strength and kindness appear to be two values held by B. in fairly constant relationship to each other in a variety of situations. Thus B. rewards and punishes his son, Maurice, 6, according to explicit rules. Transgression of a rule sometimes evokes punishment of a bread-and-water diet for half a day, or several hours in a closet. For making good grades in school, Maurice is rewarded at family meals with improvised ceremonies. B. lets him wear his own military medals, puts him by his side at the head of the table, and offers candy. Switch the scene to the factory, and the observer finds parallel situations with workers, even though the manifestations are different.'

work against the Germans.[13] The villagers took pride in belonging to a place to which one of their own, now a successful *patron* in Paris, remained loyal – a place to which his presence brought embellishment, a subject of talk and friendly gossip, and the fascination of family funerals.[14]

C. REDUCING THE WEIGHT OF THE OBLIGATION

With the above review of some of the social and cultural sources of B.'s habits of give and take in his home environment, I have tried to give the background for his ambivalence and discomfort when he became an industrial pupil of the Americans. In what ways did B. attempt to maintain self-respect and reduce the weight of his felt obligation?

B.'s psychological preparation for becoming a pupil-recipient included numerous references to the historical contributions of France to the United States. He reminded me in 1951, shortly after receiving his summons to serve as chief of a productivity mission, that France was the first nation to recognize American independence after the revolt of the colonies against Britain; that French capital, science, and technology had been important in the economic development of the new country; and that, above all, France had equipped the United States with the symbol of its mission in the world, the Statue of Liberty. These statements were the first of a series, over a period of nine years, that revealed the strivings of one recipient of American gifts to find a release from dependency feelings[15] by reminding an American of American debts to France and to express hostility and to give advice to the United States through a face-to-face relationship with a citizen of that country.[16]

13. The martyred sister remained, for B., the inspiration for many of his efforts to make France stronger and more productive through 'applying his American lessons in productivity.' He was paying her back for her personal sacrifice, her death for France. A thousand copies of a book were published as a memorial to her in March 1951.

14. Monsieur B.'s mother, who used to spend summers with her two children in the village, coming from Paris, was buried there on April 1, 1952, alongside her husband and facing a plaque dedicated to her martyred daughter whose remains were never returned from the German camp at Ravensbrück, Austria, where she died on March 25, 1945.

15. For a more generalized description of how persons, tribal groups, and nations resist dependency situations, see the speculative essay, 'Contribution à une sociologie de la dépendance,' by the French ethnologist, Georges Balandier, in *Cahiers Internationaux de Sociologie*, Vol. XII, 1952, pp. 47-69.

16. Examining the interview situation as a form of reciprocity and gift exchange, Rosalie Hankey Wax wrote in *Human Organization*: 'The gifts with which a field worker repays the efforts of his informant will vary, of course, with each investiga-

Such mixed feelings were fairly general in France in the 1950's, decreasing in proportion to the sense of self-direction and independence symbolized by: (a) the 'unauthorized' effort of France to invade Suez in October 1956, (b) the return of General de Gaulle to power, and (c) the explosion of French atomic devices in the Sahara in 1960, a success achieved without direct assent or assistance from the United States. These external events, to be described in the next chapter, are anticipated at this point in order to underscore the consistent pattern of resistance to dependence and obligations expressed by the informant during the period of the study. In B.'s own words, we can find the start of 'obligation avoidance behavior' from the outset of the American teacher-donor relationship with the French pupil-recipient:

You Americans have been using France as a buffer, a line of protection, during two wars, and now you are making ready for us to serve the same purpose against the Russians in the next world war... If it had not been for these previous wars, we would have no need to take advantage of your generosity; we have suffered death and destruction and a disruption of our economy, and a temporary removal from scientific research, but we will come back.[17]

B. had support for his views in academic circles. That is, those portions of his views that played down potential French indebtedness and dependence and emphasized the self-interest motives of Americans in making offers also were found in the writings of François Pérroux. A French economist, Pérroux has been the main student of Mauss' ideas in the context of contemporary economics. He wrote in 1954:

The Marshall Plan gifts had a coolly calculated business operation for their avowed social object. They were a purchase of security (the prevention of communist subversion), influence, and customers, over a period and in ways which are frequently indirect... They were based on comprehensive and collective calculations that underlie loans of a private kind. They involved, without the familiar conditions, chains of positive economic consequences, and thus recall to our attention a phenomenon that characterized the bulk of inter-

---

tion ...' adding that 'the interview gives informants who think themselves wronged or oppressed a change to express their grievances.'
17. These remarks, made to me in a November 1951 interview, were prompted by B.'s examination of a French pamphlet, a translation of a report written for the U.S. Government, on weaknesses of French productivity as seen by Americans. See *La Faiblesse de la productivité vue par les Américains* (Paris: Syndicat Général des Fondeurs de France), June 16, 1950. B.'s eventual report to his own industry on his American voyage printed, as frontispiece, a montage of photographs of French factories in ruins at the moment of the 1944-45 liberation. I do not mean to leave the impression that B. blamed Americans for the wars, but that the United States had failed to give France credit for her contributions in life and natural resources.

national loans of the nineteenth century, on which neither the service charges nor reimbursement of the capital sum have ever been completely accomplished – a portion of which have nevertheless, fulfilled their economic purpose.[18]

In analyzing the 'unfree' nature of the Marshall Plan gifts, Pérroux quoted a declaration of an American administrator before a convention of American bankers: 'The Marshall Plan . . . is strictly a business proposition.' Pérroux calculated that the total of Marshall Plan aid to Western Europe (April 1948-December 1952) amounted to $13,812 million, of which gifts accounted for $10,991 million, say 79.5 percent.[19] In business circles anywhere, Pérroux stated, 'gifts to customers have the increase of the firm's profit as their expressed social aim. Such gifts are directed toward important businessmen and consumers . . . This type of gift is a purchase of allies, influence, additional customers, or the loyalty of customers already won.'

Whatever motives were attributed by the French to Americans in making gifts of knowledge, B. and his productivity team became pupils of the Americans for six weeks. They accepted the gifts and asked for more as time went on. Their period of preparation to become pupils was longer than the six weeks in the United States. Then there was a period of 'continuation learning' after their return to France. The honors and privileges accorded to the mission members, in their roles as guests, failed to hide the hierarchical differences between the French pupils and their American teachers. One indicator of B.'s feeling that he was reduced in status, partly because he felt he was being put back to an earlier age level, came in his remarks at an orientation lecture just before his departure. He was told that American businessmen often return to school. For example, a familiar sight in Cambridge, Massachusetts, might be that of a head of an industry being driven, in a Cadillac, by his wife and children to a summer course for executives at Harvard Business School. He said:

In France, this could not happen. We receive such discipline in our schools, and have such an excellent preparation for life, that there is no need for adults to return to school, especially if one is already established (arrivé).

Further evidence that the American experience violated French notions of social rank and age-grading rules came from a qualified observer, Dr. Genevieve d'Haucourt, a French woman who acted as a language interpreter for several productivity teams in the United States. Also a student of anthropology, she gave this account of the French voyage:

18. FRANÇOIS PÉRROUX, 'The Gift: Its Economic Meaning in Contemporary Capitalism,' *Diogenes*, No. 7 (Summer 1954), pp. 2-3.
19. *Ibid.*, p. 2.

American hosts identified the visitors with . . . the stranger in quest of Americanization, with the newcomers in a community of equals to whom the old-timers must give a handshake. Industrialists . . . were inspired to cooperate with the aid program as neighbors, colleagues, equals . . . In France, if one has to turn toward benefactors, it is the government; this had a stigma for people coming from the middle classes, from which most of the productivity mission members were recruited. So this aid struck the recipients as a stigma of inferiority . . . Public attitudes have changed much since the war, but there remain profound traces of technical assistance being perceived as placing the visitors in an inferior and humiliating position.[20]

D'Haucourt also took note of French and American differences regarding the social position of men of knowledge and the types of knowledge on which status is based.[21] These views help us to understand another social dimension in the transmission of knowledge from Americans to Frenchmen. She wrote:

Instruction and information in the U.S. are not distinguished by defined frontiers; they are presented as sticking essentially to the facts and applicable rules. Knowledge is not prized of itself, but as a means to action. The industrialist as a man of action is superior to that of the school master or savant. The man who knows, the expert, is an auxiliary and subordinate to the chief of enterprise . . . Different from all of this is the European classic education which forms a spirit of knowledge of primary givens, of large principles of judgment. Knowledge of facts is episodic and secondary . . . While American schools verify knowledge by objective tests, European schools give their students dissertations . . . On the other side, in France, adults are believed to have passed school age. For an adult to return to school, figuratively, is a subject of mockeries, derogatory to his age. Superiority of age carries with it the superiority of knowledge; he does not add to knowledge, but his knowledge is ripened by experience.[22]

Upon his return to France, B. made frequent reference to the youthfulness

20. See her analysis, 'Some Difficulties due to Cultural Differences Shown in Technical Assistance Missions,' paper (mimeographed) read at the International Congress of Anthropology, Philadelphia, September 14, 1956. From this paper and earlier conversations with the author, I found additional support for a point already made: despite strong values of individualism in France, the productivity mission members felt strongly identified with the French state and therefore made little distinction between self and nation while abroad as emissaries and pupils. 'The strong ambivalence,' she said, 'is strongest when the French look upon technical assistance as a channel of education. The French resist a hierarchical relationship between the teacher-taught position, feeling that this places them automatically in an inferior position. National honor is at stake,' she said.

21. Cf. FLORIAN ZNANIECKI, *The Social Role of the Man of Knowledge* (New York: Columbia University Press, 1940), pp. 23-90.

22. D'HAUCOURT, *op. cit.*, passim.

of American managers and engineers in high places and their lack of preparedness to assume professorial roles even about matters in which they were undoubtedly specialized. The 'child-like' qualities of Americans were mentioned repeatedly and, in the final report to his industry, the following characterization was printed under the general heading, 'Les Hommes':

The American is young, for he faces life with curiosity, with a desire to learn, a desire to progress. These are attributes of youth. He is equally young in the sense that he is gay, likable, and that he has a general manner of desiring, very sincerely, to help others.[23]

Though the pupils praised their teachers for their generosity and willingness to share what the pupils would have considered industrial secrets, there was considerable evidence that French visitors, in accepting instruction so generously given, had not been prepared for two characteristics they later attributed to their American teachers: a) Americans' ignorance of their historical debts to European technology, and b) their lack of interest in any recent experience of French science and technology which might aid the Americans in the improvement of their industry. For B. reported:

Americans could not have been more generous with their time and good will (*bonne volonté*), but my mission members found it curious that not one American asked us about any of the French developments in synthetics or plastics. True, they talked of our historic friendship, and France as a second home of Americans, but not once did we hear any questions about *our* inventions. Perhaps Americans feel they are too advanced . . .[24]

Granting a variety of reasons why the American gifts were highly valued by the French team, B. and D., the two chief spokesmen for the mission, frequently discussed the great stimulus the voyage would bring to French industry as well as contribute to social harmony in France.[25] With each

23. In order not to identify the individuals and the team about which this study is written, I am omitting here a reference to the published report from which I have translated this passage. An examination of various French productivity reports and travel diaries by French novelists and essayists, however, will show how widespread is a French impression that Americans live in a youth culture. One example is JAQUES FREYMOND, 'America in European Eyes,' *The Annals*, Vol. 295 (September 1954), pp. 33-41.
24. Interviews, March 1952. Similar comments were repeated in October 1954 and July 1956.
25. Some recent evidence that the French economy responded to a variety of stimuli in the 1950's is found in the following newspaper dispatch from Paris: 'In 1960 France paid off $ 468,500,000 in foreign debt, almost $ 190,000,000 of it *in advance of due dates* [italics mine] . . . Since January, 1959 . . . the index for hourly

expression of gratitude for the chance to 'prime the French pump,' however, there were complaints extending the earlier themes, that a) the Americans ignored not only the French contributions to world technology, but the heavy French national expenditures going into technical assistance directly and through the United Nations to African countries, and b) the inability of their American teachers to explain productivity in any broader terms than engineers' definitions of units of work per man-hour.

These were the reactions of adults no longer familiar with the childhood roles of learning and receiving; their personal and national pride was hurt; generosity was proving uncomfortable. The failure of Americans to provide the French with cues as to how they might reciprocate served only to heighten the hierarchical difference between teacher and pupil and donor and receiver. The Marshall Plan experiences of Frenchmen served as a trigger, by 1952, to set off a series of self-assurances that were symptomatic of reactions to conquest and nativistic revivals in pre-industrial societies.[26] These self-assurances could be paraphrased as: 'We French have a unique civilization and a set of intellectual and scientific achievements of which we need not be ashamed.' In reacting to the new influences from abroad, B. at first singled out the intellectual differences between American and French engineers. We described his and others' reactions as follows:

Americans seemed not to understand our questions even when we spoke to them in good English. For example, I asked an engineer in Akron, 'What is

---

wages has gone from 128.6 to 143 for an 11 per cent gain ... A comparison index showing the ratio of wages to prices stood at 105.5 in 1960, the most favorable level for wage earners in the past five years.' Reported by ROBERT C. DOTY, 'France Answers the Trade Challenge,' *New-York Times*, January 10, 1961, p. 49 *et seq.* These economic statistics are interesting for at least two reasons in the light of this investigation: a) the repayment of foreign debts is another indication of the nation acting according to my informants' desire to find freedom and autonomy by eliminating obligation; and b) the wage-price ratio for 1960 shows that there may have been objective consequences of American 'gifts,' specifically the economic means and managerial knowledge aimed at improving productivity so Frenchmen would have more goods at lower prices and a chance thereby to reduce class conflict by making workers less envious of their bosses. If the same class tensions exist, however, in 1961 as in 1951, they may be obscured by the cleavages represented by opposing French views on the Algerian war. These antagonisms seem not to follow clearly defined lines. The opposing views about an Algerian solution, in other words, are more complex for analysis than the social harmony which some Marshall Plan officials thought might follow improved productivity. The formula: remove conspicuous consumption of expensive goods by bosses and, with an economy of abundance, France will be free of civil strife, potential revolutions and Communists.

26. Cf. SOL TAX, ed., *Heritage of Conquest* (Glencoe: The Free Press, 1952) and A. KROEBER, *Anthropology*, new edition (New York: Harcourt, Brace and Co., 1948), pp. 437-444.

your first principle of mass production?' He hesitated and then took me to the assembly line, where he pointed to the conveyor belt and said, 'There it is.' Americans seem to talk either in generalizations or completely in examples. You can never see with them what is the main idea, the general idea first, and then have them illustrate it with a particular instance of the general idea . . . I have been exhausted every night going back to the hotel room and having to reassemble all the little pieces of information Americans have given me – the little examples – and putting them into some order.

The contrast between inductive and deductive approaches to knowledge and its transmission continued to interfere with communication between teacher and pupil after the return of the mission to France. The mission members, preparing their report, consulted Americans at their Paris offices for ideas about the classification of materials. The assumption was that U.S. consultants, having had experience with other French teams reporting on their trips, could advise on the most effective ways to describe American techniques. B. said:

We finally had to abandon these inquiries. It was difficult to make ourselves understood. The Americans are more Cartesian than the French, always wanting to deal with concrete reality . . . We are more concerned at this stage (1952) with the general schema, and we are deciding that the French know better than the Americans how to present the idea of productivity. I think we could help the Americans explain productivity because we have had training in philosophy and can see both structure and the association of ideas in comprehending reality.[27]

The translation of the table of contents (see below) of one French publication will indicate the format which French teams considered more palatable than *une mentalité américaine* characterized as 'how-to-do-it-ism.'[28] The French, metaphorically speaking, received a gift unwrapped, and they decided to add value to it (for themselves) by wrapping it properly. In this

27. The French philosopher of productivity, Jean Fourastié, a graduate of Ecole Centrale, the same institution attended by B., eventually took note of the view expressed first by B. and later by this investigator in an article, 'L'aide spirituelle française peut résoudre six crises américaines,' *Documents* (Paris), No. 108, February 1957, pp. 9-14. Fourastié quoted the article in his book, *Révolution à l'ouest* (Paris: Presses Universitaires de France, 1957), p. 4 (co-author, A. Laleuf).

28. See PIERRE BADIN, ed., *Aux sources de la Productivité américaine* (Paris: Association Française pour l'Accroissement de la Productivité, 1953). Translation mine. This report, presented by a French law professor, corresponds to a style not to be distinguished from reports written by engineers or parliamentarians, all products of French education. For contrasts in styles of presentation of ideas about productivity in reports written by Germans, Americans, and Frenchmen, see articles listed in *Bibliography on Productivity* (Paris: Organization of European Economic Cooperation, 1956), p. 250.

process, the value was in the intellectual exercise itself; the possession of the gift then became of value because they had added something to it, had made it ornamental.[29]

Summary of *At the Sources of American Productivity*, Published in 1953 under auspices of the French Association for the Increase of Productivity.

Preface
Introduction

General Factors
First part:
1. The United States, Economic Aristocracy
2. The Extension of the Market
3. American Mentality
4. Credit and Means of Financing the Enterprise
5. Fiscality
6. Economic Documentation
7. Free Competition

Technical Factors
Second part:
1. Market Research
2. Standardization
3. Specialization and Mass Production
4. Localization of Establishments
5. The Localization of Sites of Plants
6. Mechanization
7. Scientific Research
8. Quality of Finished Products
9. Delivery

29. Analysis of the finished reports of other missions reveals the sources of frustration Frenchmen felt in their search for ready-made, well articulated principles of productivity which could be put in their reports. America was, in perceptual terms, 'an unstructured situation' and Americans were thought not to be cooperative in giving the structure the French wanted. The French seemed unable to find 'closure' in the sense of *gestalt* psychology. The reports are highly schematic, unfailingly uniform in style of presentation. Such headings as 'human, technical and environmental factors of productivity' usually appear in some sequence in the reports. From a functional point of view, these culturally induced needs for structural clarity seem not unlike the manifestations Balinese give for needing to know the location of *kaja*, the center of the island, as a point of personal orientation. *Kaja* has been described by Margaret Mead in her paper, 'Cultural Transformations in Ecological Perspective,' read before the meeting of the American Association for the Advancement of Science, New York, December 28, 1956.

69

10. Preparation and Organization of Work
11. Reduction of Handling
12. Accounting: Measure and Factory of Productivity
13. Organization of Distribution and Sales Promotion

Human Factors
Third part:
 1. The Mystique of Service
 2. The Social Climate
 3. Trade Unions and the Enterprise
 4. Human Relations
 5. Public Relations
 6. Sharing Responsibility
 7. Formation and Improvement of Managers
 8. Apprenticeship
 9. Professional Selection
10. The Call to Worker Initiative
11. Job Evaluation and Merit Rating
12. Faithfulness to Classical Modes of Renumerating Work
13. America Discovers Proportional Salary
14. The Adoption of the Sliding Scale by General Motors
15. Participation in Benefits by Workers
16. High Salaries, Cause and Consequence of Productivity
17. Living Standards

Conclusion

Summary
Going back to the stated purpose of this study in the introduction, let us recall these objectives in the light of the material presented in this chapter. The case of Monsieur B. gives credence to Mauss' generalizations about the universality of types of obligation found among ancient and primitive people. I have tried to show that such types of obligation also are at work in modern industrial societies (giving, receiving, and repaying). Technical assistance rather than ceremonial gift exchange is the framework for these transactions. In this chapter the focus has been on one of the three types of obligation, *the obligation to receive.* A Frenchman, with both unique and universal traits, has shown psychological responses (to playing the recipient's role) that are remindful of donor-receiver relationships in simpler societies. Old problems are turning up in new guises. One problem of industrial men in the Atlantic community, no less than in Melanesia or the Northwest American coast, is how the recipients of gifts can maintain dignity while waiting for the opportunity to liquidate their culturally-

phrased and determined feelings of indebtedness and obligation. In B. we have a study of ambivalence. Lacking an institutionalized or ceremonial means of restoring his status as a donor, B. represents one instance in a larger case of Frenchmen whose initial reactions were to deprecate the value of the gift and question the motives of the donor. The weight of the obligation was reduced by challenging the magnanimity of the donor and by seeking as yet undiscovered ways to make a return gift.

Knowledge, like inherited family silver, masks, paintings, or tools, can be transformed during its possession by the recipient. While tangible goods may take on new forms or shapes or increase in sentimental and monetary value, intellectual goods are subject to synthesis and reclassification. The gift is put, so to speak, in a new package. Whether first accepted joyfully or reluctantly, the gift, if improved or transformed through its care and nurture by the recipient, becomes a commodity with the *potential* value of going back to the donor as a return gift. The French, heirs to deductive, Cartesian styles of thought, worked out, for their own purposes of understanding, a codification of the American idea of productivity. If social arrangements could be invented to permit intellectual gifts to flow back in the direction of the donor, who now would be under an obligation to receive, the recipients could return to their original roles as donors and teachers and dignity would be restored.

Until technical assistance processes can be found to handle all three types of obligation, recipients, as I shall show in the next chapter, will find other 'compensatory mechanisms' for discharging felt obligations.

CHAPTER IV

THE OBLIGATION TO REPAY

'In primitive or archaic types of society,' Mauss asked, 'what is the principle whereby the gift received has to be repaid? What force is there in the thing given which compels the recipient to make a return?'[1]

We come now to the third of the three types of obligation which Mauss considered as universal to the gift exchange practices and institutions covered in his studies: the obligation to repay gifts. As in the previous two chapters, Mauss is again recalled for his statement that 'everything is stuff to be given away and repaid.'[2] Another phrasing of this point, adapted from Herskovits,[3] is the following proposition: *Gifts demand countergifts. No matter how freely*[4] *a gift may be tendered, or how unsought it may be, the very fact of its having been given or presented carries an obligation of some kind of return that can be ignored only on*

1. M. MAUSS, *The Gifts*, p. 1.
2. *Ibid.*, p. 12.
3. The phrasing of this proposition is an interpretation of Mauss' ideas by Melville Herskovits in his discussion of gift and ceremonial exchange in *Economic Anthropology* (New York: Knopf, 1952), p. 155.
4. My field work gave me a new understanding of the dialogue between Mauss and Malinowski about free gifts and unfree gifts. Mauss criticized Malinowski's earlier interpretations of 'the pure gift' among the Trobriands, a criticism Malinowski later reached independently and then acknowledged. Mauss challenged the notion that gifts could be 'free' or 'pure.' B. MALINOWSKI, *Crime and Custom in Savage Society* (New York: Humanities Press, 1951), pp. 40-41. The data of my study suggest that the Americans, as donors, and the French, as recipients, both showed signs of mixed feelings about giving and receiving. American government officials wavered between a desire to consider their gifts as freely given, and, at the same time, a desire to see themselves as unsentimental, calculating, and tough, acting in the nation's enlightened self-interest. Similarly, the French suspecting the motives of the donor, could accept more willingly therefore the obligations to receive and pay back because the gift was *not* pure. Knowing that the donors were benefiting by the gift helped reduce somewhat their loss of dignity and prestige in their own eyes.

penalty of social disapprobation and the loss of prestige. Psychologically, this holds for all cultures.[5]

A corollarly to this proposition is: if national status is maintained by giving rather than hoarding, people in the donor nation are likely to be unaware of, or to ignore, the efforts of those in the debtor nation to originate action by giving gifts to those above them. Whether through indifference, innocence, or a conscious effort to preserve status by refusing to accept gifts, the donor nation incurs the hostility[6] of people in the receiver nation to the extent that the donor frustrates the discharge of their felt obligation.

With these generalizations in mind, I wish to review the strains in such a donor-receiver relationship which appeared when B. found himself without a satisfactory ceremonial or other means to discharge his felt obligation and to be accepted as an equal. In what personal and international events can we find symptoms of frustrated gift behavior on the part of my informant and some of his countrymen? How did he seek reciprocity and esteem for himself and France? What can be considered as psychological alternatives to countergifts?[7]

5. Ruth Benedict has contributed to this point by her analysis of the countergift in Japanese culture. She compares Japanese, New Guinean, and Melanesian processes of 'clearing one's name' in *The Chrysanthemum and the Sword* (Boston: Houghton-Mifflin Co., 1946), pp. 145-176. Wardle states: 'It is the law of the gift that it may not be summarily refused without giving offense, and a counter gift must be tendered in due season.' See H. N. WARDLE, 'Gifts,' *Encyclopedia of the Social Sciences* (New York, Macmillan Co., 1931), Vol. III, pp. 657-658. He referred to: a) the Maori practice of classifying with theft the failure to offer the return gift; b) a comparison between the transfer of blazoned mats in Samoa and return gifts in ancient Irish custom; and c) countergifts of North Africans invited to circumcision and marriage feasts. 'What is called marriage by purchase,' he wrote, 'is often in fact gift and countergift, for the women whose parents do not make satisfactory return gifts may be sent back.' *Ibid.*, pp. 657-658.

6. Mauss dealt only implicitly with cases of hostility against donors who prevent recipients from making countergifts. He said of the Kwakiutl potlatch: 'Sometimes there is no question of receiving return; one destroys simply in order to give the appearance that one has no desire to receive anything back.' Borrowing from all his sources, however, he concluded: 'Much of our everyday morality is concerned with the question of obligation and the spontaneity of the gift ... The gift not yet repaid debases the man who accepted it, particularly if he did so without thought of return ... charity wounds him who receives, and our whole moral effort is directed toward suppressing the *unconscious* harmful patronage of the rich almoner.'

7. This phrase is made with apologies to William James for his essay, 'The Moral equivalent of War.' Cf. RALPH BARTON PERRY, *The Thought and Character of William James* (New York: George Braziller, 1954), p. 229. For a more recent discussion of 'compensatory mechanism,' cf. ALVIN GOULDNER, 'Reciprocity and Autonomy in Functional Theory,' in L. GROSS, ed., *Symposium on Sociological Theory* (Evanston and White Plains: Row, Peterson & Co., 1959), p. 249. He wrote: '... Any

The main outline of answers to these questions has been sketched in the introduction where, for the sake of brevity, both macro- and microcosmic events were presented in schematic form under the heading, 'The French Quest for Autonomy and Reciprocity.' Now let us amplify some of the points in that account of one case study of the international giving, receiving, and repaying process.

In the macrocosm, there were the depressed economic conditions in Europe inspiring Americans to create the Marshall Plan and the French to accept their place in the orbit of American philanthropy.[8] Against this backdrop of geopolitical events (war, American-led alliances, and the search for raw materials), B. used the interview situation with an American investigator in Paris as a safety-value through which to express and act out his grievances.[9] B. wanted American help. However, he felt the

---

structure is more likely to exist if it is engaged in reciprocally functional inter-changes with some others; the less reciprocal the functional interchange between structures, the less likely is either structure, or the patterned relationship between them, to persist – unless compensatory mechanisms are present.'

8. 'The generosity and political disinterestedness which inspired the Marshall Plan were unable to resist the wear and tear of daily political life (in Europe),' wrote Salvador de Madariaga in an analysis of 'Why Americans Are Unpopular.' See *World Liberalism*, Vol. 7, No. 2, Summer 1957, p. 18.) He objected to the notion that there could be 'aid without strings,' noting that '... gifts with advice, in the eyes of the recipients, are apt to look very much like orders.' In suggesting how natural it was for 'anti-gratitude' to develop among people who receive, he said '... the benefactor was soon found irksome and cumbersome. Every one of his deeds was a reminder of his superiority. This kind of thing is difficult for individuals to swallow; for nations it is quite impossible.' (*Ibid.*, p. 16.)

9. Cf. RHODA MÉTRAUX, 'A Note on the Spectator in French Culture,' in MARGARET MEAD and RHODA MÉTRAUX, *op. cit.*, for an intriguing clue to interpreting B.'s use of the interview situation to demonstrate to himself and me that he could be again an active donor with an American as a receiver. Out of a range of highly stylized French ways to be both an active and passive spectator or apprentice, B. chose the active role in which he could exercise choice and judgment. While in the U.S., he had little chance, he complained, to speak; he was generally the passive, silent, sub-ordinate listener-apprentice. Back in France, in a face-to-face relationship with an American, he could feel participation and a personal control and direction lacking when he was a laissez-faire spectator of American industry. I, the American, became subordinate, the passive audience, and he became superordinate and exhibitionist. His country and mine functioned occasionally as 'the third person' in what normally was the type of 'exclusive dyadic relationship' typical of French culture (cf. *ibid.*, p. 391). At moments when we were not perceived by each other as the personifica-tion of a whole nation, we were 'the quiet spectators' of the interaction between other actors (nations), i.e., commenting with detachment sometimes on the follies or strengths of an Eisenhower or a de Gaulle. In such a relationship, amounting to

'penalty of social disapprobation and loss of prestige' by taking a role placing him and France in a subservient position so that money, machines, food, and advice flowed in downward direction. A weaker, smaller France, also a teacher-donor nation, accepted such gifts from the technologically stronger United States and with improved economic strength in the 1950's, showed signs of restoring *grandeur*. B. then, in interviews,[10] both re-stated past grievances against the donor and expressed satisfaction when France, without American superversion or consent a) sent military forces into Suez, b) restored de Gaulle to power as a strong leader promising France great power status,[11] and c) developed and exploded atomic devices-against the wishes of a donor nation which had refused France a request for nuclear secrets.

The above events helped B., by talking about them to an American, to feel that France again was making a contribution to the Western world by being herself again, realizing her historic mission of giving and teaching.[12]

---

fictitious kinship, hostility could be expressed by a Frenchman as a sign of intimacy. We were both spectators – sometimes active, sometimes passive – before the drama of a cold war which forced our countries to attempt an uneasy and awkward effort at mutuality.

10. The psychoanalytic concept of transference is partly applicable to understanding my experience with B. As a non-judging but not altogether silent listener, I received 'transfers' of feelings developed out of a lifetime of reciprocal situations which B. found lacking in his teacher-taught, donor-receiver relations with Americans. Here I am using transference merely in the interpersonal situation (observer-observed, investigator-informant) and without the nuances of Freud who dealt with the unseen, the unconscious manifest in recall of dreams. Cf. A. A. BRILL, *The Basic Writings of Sigmund Freud* (New York: Modern Library, 1938), p. 537. Cf. also HENRY L. LEENARD, ARNOLD BERNSTEIN *et al.*, *The Anatomy of Psychotherapy: Systems of Communication and Expectation* (New York: Columbia University Press, 1960). Leenard, in private communication, has told me that some psychiatrists and patients speak of exchanging intangible gifts (e.g., self-knowledge).

11. De Gaulle's dramatic return to power is comparable to 'nativistic revival' tendencies found in simpler societies reacting to conquest. See A. L. KROEBER, *Anthropology* (New York: Harcourt, Brace & Co., 1948), p. 437, for his discussion of nativism, revivals, and messiahs. Especially interesting is a comparison between de Gaulle and a primitive contemporary, Paliau (Cf. MARGARET MEAD, *New Lives For Old* (New York: William Morrow and Co., 1956), pp. 188-211), 'whose imagination turned unfocused postwar discontent into a full-fledged political movement . . . who had a program for action, an organized picture of change which involved genuine ethical ideals . . . he wanted all the people to become one people, eschew narrow rivalries . . . pooling their specialized skills and possessions.'

12. This *mission civilisatrice* was strongly felt by B. as he presided over potlatch-type family feasts, with me as a guest, and during the times he escorted me to see Napoleon's tomb and the Versailles palace. He reflected a point of view expressed by a French government official arguing for a greater budget for overseas cultural activities in 1920: 'Our letters, our arts, our intellectual civilization, our ideas, have

The statements of hostility toward the donor were coupled with French efforts to win the approval of the donor – for lessons well learned and gifts put into use – and to give Americans instructions in Moslem psychology. Together, these reactions were imperfect substitutes for counter-gifts, but they helped B. to carry out his obligation to repay. He found these unplanned countergifts more satisfactory than what Americans apparently expected: gratitude, affection, anti-Communist votes, and permission to build military installations and station troops.

To give some substance to the above generalizations, I have chosen four examples of B.'s efforts to handle the obligation to make a return of some kind to the United States. The first deals with his desire to give political education to Americans in exchange for their technological knowledge. That the Americans were by-passing France to establish direct relationships with North African nationalists was a persistent charge during the nine years covered in this study. The trouble was that Americans would not listen to French advice on how to deal with Moslem Africa.

First example

B. assert on September 12, 1956:

I would like to give Foster Dulles a whole box of Korans and request that he and President Eisenhower read them every morning . . . The United States is playing a dangerous game in Egypt and in the rest of North Africa, and this is because you know nothing of the Islamic religion . . . Allah loves strong men, and you are making the Occident look weak in the eyes of the Moslems . . . America may dazzle the world with her productivity, but it is plain she has a lot to learn from us about the need to show strength before Moslems . . . A *marabou* can become easily a commissar.

Lacking a channel to the U.S. Government, B. requested that I write articles and make speeches about the 'folly of American foreign policy' upon my return to the United States so that 'your countrymen will have the benefit of what you have learned in France about Islam.'

Second example

While trying to give Americans advice and instruction about Moslem culture, B. and other Frenchman sought gifts as well. They wanted atomic secrets. We refer, of course, to knowledge regarded by the U.S. as secret in the interests of national survival. The American donors had given technological knowledge to the French with a degree of freedom that surprised the recipients who, by their standards, would have feared such a loss of industrial secrets. But the American donors hoarded some knowledge as

---

always had a powerful attraction for foreign nations.' See RUTH MCMURRY and MUNA LEE, *The Cultural Approach* (Chapel Hill: University of North Carolina Press, 1947), p. 17.

76

though the knowledge consisted of family secrets or tribal lore,[13] the sharing of which would mean loss of honor or loss of power. The United States thus contributed to be ambivalence of French feelings by selecting knowledge which would be given and by hoarding knowledge which, in U.S. national interest, could not be shared even with friends or allies.

The French made consistent efforts to request that Americans share with them the benefits of scientific research on atomic energy. The refusal of the request implied distrust and added a second source of humiliation for the French, already suffering from dependence and the effects of unfulfilled obligations.[14] The refusal produced vows to create such knowledge without outside assistance and then to use such knowledge as a source of power for bargaining. As Mauss pointed out, 'Failure to give or to receive, like failure to make a return gift, means a loss of dignity.'[15]

B., hearing of my previous residence in Japan, took this as his cue to make a series of statements of reproach about the United States' policies on atomic energy. In 1952 he spoke of the well-publicized American destruction of Japan's cyclotron,[16] an event of 1945 dictated by Occupa-

---

13. Scarce knowledge of the type associated with nuclear fission is subject to controls of the law of supply and demand, like any other commodity exchanged in economic institutions. Reciprocity rules seem less demanding when the knowledge is perceived as a source of indispensable power, and cannot be given or sold. Psychologically, strains develop between the petitioner and the possesssor if the possessor has already given other gifts in the name of friendship. The human organization invented by Americans to control the distribution of such knowledge (classification systems with penalties, oaths, etc.) are comparable to interaction restrictions in secret societies and sodalities. Cf. C. CHAPPLE and C. COON, *Principles of Anthropology* (New York: Henry Holt, 1942), p. 422; and ROBERT LOWIE, *Social Organization* (New York: Rinehart, 1948), pp. 294-316. The classic use of spies to overcome such restrictions of knowledge is described in a popular history of espionage, RONALD SETH, *Spies At Work* (New York: Philosophical Library, 1954), p. 231.

14. The important point here is the psychological reaction against the gift withheld. It is outside the scope of this study to report the actual U.S. and French government negotiations and policies related to (a) U.S. restrictions, and (b) French scientific and political policies represented by the Euratom community and the eventual Sahara explosion on February 13, 1960. The refusal functioned as a block to French efforts to improve their position in the hierarchy of nations and represented American indifference to reciprocity.

15. *The Gift*, p. 40.

16. The intensity of Japanese intellectuals' reactions to the destruction of the cyclotron at Tokyo University was almost comparable to the original shock of the actual bombs at Hiroshima and Nagasaki, and it remained such a sore point that, in order to re-establish rapport between Japanse intellectuals and Western Christianity, a compensatory gift was offered by American Episcopalians in 1958. A reactor has been installed at St. Paul's University, Tokyo. The Society of Jesus, coincidentally, has been the donor of Africa's first atomic reactor, a propitiatory gift of knowledge and prestige, from Belgian Jesuits to the University of Lovanium in the Congo.

tion authorities as assurance that the Japanese would not possess knowledge necessary to wage war again. In 1954 and 1956 he referred to the
mutilated Japanese cyclotron again as an example of what America was
doing symbolically to the French efforts to 'join the atomic club.' He said
in July 1956:

You might as well be using axes against us by your refusal to have our
scientists join together in atomic research ... This is especially odious to us
considering American debts to French science, and the fact that you apparently
trust the British more than you do the French by exchanging atomic information with them.

Third example

The most striking example of French hostility toward their protector-
benefactors, growing out of the conditions described above, concerns the
Suez affair of 1956 and subsequent French reactions to American efforts
to stop British, French, and Israeli intervention in a crisis prompted by the
closing of the Suez canal by President Nasser of Egypt. On October 31,
1956 France and Britain joined Israel in preparing to send armed forces
to Suez. The United States government was not informed in advance.[17]
This independent action provided a psychological release for the French,[18]
since it seemed to give them a renewed sense of autonomy and self-direc-

17. Manifestations against the action took various forms in the United States: 1)
Secretary of State Dulles, according to the Alsop columnists in the November 3,
1956, issue of the *New York Herald Tribune,* called the French ambassador, Hervé
Alphand, and 'gave him the kind of lecture that an old-fashioned schoolmaster might
give to a juvenile delinquent ... ;' 2) James Reston, reporting to the *New York
Times* from Washington the same day, said: 'So sharp and strong were the feelings
about the British-French policy of force that the crisis in the Western alliance overshadowed even the grave events of the Middle East;' and 3) General James Van Fleet,
former United Nations commander in Korea, according to the United Press, said:
'the action of Britain, France and Israel was "the meanest thing any ally who has
received our money could possibly do to Uncle Sam." '
18. For a discussion of the significance of safety-value events or institutions, see
Coser's analysis of a proposition by Georg Simmel: '... the opposition of a member
to an associate is no purely negative social factor, if only because such opposition is
often the only means for making life with actually unbearable people at least possible.' (LEWIS COSER, *The Functions of Social Conflict* (Glencoe: Free Press, 1956),
p. 39.) Of this, Coser wrote: 'Conflict ... "clears the air," i.e., it eliminates the accumulation of blocked and balked hostile dispositions by allowing their free behavioral expression. Simmel echoes Shakespeare's King John: "So foul a sky clears not
without a storm." ' Coser notes also that Simmel writing before he knew about the
new psychoanalytic theories in Vienna, 'did not conceive of the possibilities that in
cases in which conflict behavior against the original object is blocked 1) hostile feelings may be deflected upon substitute objects and that 2) substitute satisfaction may
be obtained through mere tension release.' *Ibid.,* p. 40.

78

tion and, hypothetically, was a countergift of revenge against the Americans who had refused to accept their gifts of knowledge about 'the best way to deal with Moslems.'

On January 9, 1957, B. read on the front page of *Le Figaro* an open letter to Americans written by Thierry Maulnier, French editor and writer. I received a copy of it along with a personal letter from B. Excerpts from both will illustrate attitudes of persons in a nation which has experienced 'wounds of charity' and has suffered from what the receivers regarded as 'too much generosity, protection,[19] and superversion.'

Maulnier wrote in his *Figaro* letter, later reproduced in the February 6, 1957 issue of the *New York Times*:

So the Algerian problem is not going to be put before the U.N.O. . . . We are told that your Government . . . will decide, not unsadly, to take sides against us, being unable to cause the slightest pain to its new pan-Arab friends . . . We will not even talk of gratitude, if you please; *it is well known that gratitude is hardly a political value* [italics mine] . . . Anti-American feeling does exist in France . . . You are very rich, very powerful, very effective, you play in the world a dominant role . . . We suffer from weaknesses and, as is only natural, we tend to fall back on those qualities we can still keep . . . The Franco-American friendship is in danger . . . It is not so certain that you have acted rightly when you filled the Nasser balloon with air, when you refused him a loan for Aswan and threw him back in Suez, when you paralyzed . . . the efforts we French and English made to defend our rights and our prestige, and when finally you filled again the balloon when it had been burst by the pin-prick from Israel and from us . . . *Perhaps you would be wrong to trust too much in our need of you. For this is a reciprocal need* [italics mine] . . . When one deprives an old and still proud race of what constitutes the only future worthy of its past, one runs the risk of leading it, against its own interests, perhaps, to unforseeable, impassioned outbursts.

B.'s letter, forwarding the Maulnier letter, pleaded for an American understanding of the French crisis. My translation follows:

I always want to write to you and I lack the time, but here is a *Figaro* letter which says the essentials of what we are thinking here . . . You know very well my friendship for America, and I am happy to think that a man like Truman recognizes that the United States has committed a grave fault in leaving without a sanction the 'rapt' of the Suez Canal. Today the situation is even worse: accused for having defended Suez, we are about to be accused at

19. The French Dominican priest, R. L. Bruckberger, writing in the December 27, 1956, issue of *Reporter*, proposed that the United States might play the 'liege lord of the West.' He argued that if it were not for 'the troublesome American desire to be loved by all the world,' the U.S. might honorably protect its European 'vassals' in exchange for their allegiance, and that would be an honorable arrangement for both parties.'

the U.N. by a Nehru who has in his country 80 million untouchables, and who has not accepted the U.N. decisions about Kashmir; by a Nasser, a caricature of Hitler; by Yemen which still practices slavery; by Ibn Saud who is stuffed with the dollars of Aramco, etc., etc. We have no lessons to receive from people like that! The Algerian problem is our problem and our error – if it is one – is to have permitted 2 million inhabitants of becoming 10 million, instead of adopting the method of the United States as regards the Indians, who are no more than several hundred thousand ... Pope Pius XII in his Christmas message spoke of two weights and two measures of the U.N. To America we say it is necessary to choose between friends of the North Atlantic organization and those whom you believe to be your new friends and who hit you in the face after having pocketed your dollars, if you continue to show the same weakness as you have shown since the start of the crisis ... I do not wish to cry with my heart, but we live here in anguish and fear that this time again America understands *too late*.

The Atlantic alliance persisted in 1961. It is beyond this analysis to suggest the process by which compensatory mechanisms operated to allow it to hold together. From B.'s reactions, which I believe to have been widely shared by other members of the French *bourgeoisie*, one might conclude that the exhilaration over acting autonomously and independently of the United States, for even a short-lived moment, constituted a 'compensatory mechanism,' a catharsis which produced feelings of self-esteem and hope that France could take once again the initiative[20] and force attention on demands to participate in decisions which affected her. The part played by France in the Suez events of October 1956 functioned as one of a series of psychological alternatives to making countergifts to the United States. Thus the French were able to pay back debts with 'revenge'

20. B., despite the rage he said he felt at alleged American efforts to block French traffic to the Suez, enjoyed a considerable increase in morale after the crisis was over. Various references were made in later interviews (1958, 1959, 1960) to those moments of glory when France was acting alone, with no entanglements with N.A.T.O. or the Americans. He conceded that such *grandeur*, de Gaulle's often-repeated slogan, was more easily found in the 19th century when France could make 'military promenades' along the Nile without creating disturbances. 'We are individualists, and do not operate well in a team (*equipe*) or an alliance,' he said. It is interesting to compare B.'s reactions with a statement by Kurt Lewin about initiative and morale: 'Initiative and productivity, dependent as they are on the proper balance of a variety of factors, are highly sensitive to changes in this balance (i.e., quality and quantity of achievement-productivity.)' Cf. his essay, 'Time Perspective and Morale,' in G. WATSON, ed., *Civilian Morale* (Boston: Houghton Mifflin, 1942). From a morale point of view, the Suez events helped B. to look backward to past French glory (e.g., the Napoleonic era) and to project such a memory into the future as a hopeful prospect. Taking the initiative again was the key to the morale he expressed for the nation. It produced for him a new balance in Franco-American relations.

advice, warnings, and instructions. As Maulnier said, France demands reciprocity in her relations with other nations.

Fourth example

Apart from B.'s and Maulnier's letters to Americans, there was other evidence to suggest that French industrialists, who represented the chief points of contact with Americans in the receiver-pupil role, were searching for recognition, by Americans, of past and potential French contributions to the welfare of Atlantic and other nations. The *Comité France Actuelle*, supported financially by French businessmen and industrialists, maintained an office in Washington, D.C., to inform Americans on French progress. One of its publications, a 1956 pamphlet, *France Means Business*, presented the image of France as a donor as well as a receiver of technical aid:

French engineers are building or advising on hundreds of projects in some 73 countries ... Highly industrialized countries like the United States, Canada, Great Britain, Germany, Sweden and Switzerland are buying the right to French products and production techniques.

The yearning for friendship on an equal partner basis was further suggested when the French businessmen spoke through *France Actuelle*:

... The world's business is a two-way street, and France, in addition to what she creates, adapts to French requirements the industrial output and know-how of the world. Thus, in France today one finds the best of American products made in French factories according to American ways. So in America one now finds American companies building factories to make French products according to French ways.

Such statements showed that the French, lacking American attention to their desire to be recognized for gifts they could offer, invented their own devices to make exchanges: demanding the chance to give as well as to receive.

B. PERSPECTIVES FROM INDUSTRIAL SOCIOLOGY

Having proposed that substitutes, even if unsatisfactory, can be found for countergifts when there are no ceremonies or institutions to take care of the receiver's obligation to repay, I wish now to look at the above events from the perspectives of research on small groups in industry. Then I will compare the technical assistance exchanges in the North Atlantic with the *kula* institution of the Melanesians to provide a primitive perspective on the French quest for reciprocity.

What behavioral elements are there in common in such different empirical contexts as the Bank Wiring Room of the Hawthorne Plant, a pajama factory in Virginia, and the Atlantic alliance? Is it possible that human aggregations offering such dramatic contrasts in size, ranging from face-to-face interactions of five working girls to a treaty coalition of nations across a wide ocean, could reflect any common characteristics? Research on behavior in industrial organization has yet to be synthesized with a theory of obligations applied to international alliances. However, Mauss would recognize, no doubt, as kindred scientific inquires such work, for example, as that of Arensberg, Tootell, Chapple and others in their search for generalizations about conditions leading to stress or equilibrium in interpersonal relations. With the French material still in mind, I wish to take up two conceptual frames, used in studies of small groups, which have relevance for diagnosing the strains in international donor-receiver relationships. They are: 1) *communication*, and 2) *leadership*.

Arensberg and Tootell, acknowledging their debts to Mayo, Whyte, Bakke, Chapple, Parsons, Merton, and Homans, wrote of communication:

... The concept of communication is useful in studies of organization. If it is through communication that any interaction (social) system is built up, then the longer and the smoother, the more satisfying and the less blocking and frustrating the communication, the more common norms appear. 'Two-way' communication, then, might afford the link between a social system and its possible eventual creation of common values.[21]

The frustrations felt by the French in the Suez events, expressed in various ways in order to move the blocks Americans innocently put in the way of their making countergifts (i.e., 'feedback'), seem to fit the above generalization as much as the earlier empirical works from which it was derived. 'Two-way communication' was lacking, from the French point of view, and France accordingly broke, temporarily, the links tying her social system to the larger system of the Atlantic alliance. The 'smoother, more satisfying' Franco-American relationship which followed, though not with-

21. See CONRAD ARENSBERG and GEOFFREY TOOTELL, 'Plant Sociology: Real Discoveries and New Problems,' in MIRRA KOMAROVSKY, ed., *Common Frontiers of the Social Sciences* (Glencoe: Free Press, 1957), p. 321. Their summary of communication and interaction theory refers to these earlier works: E. MAYO, *The Human Problems of an Industrial Civilization* (Boston: Harvard Business School (second edition), 1946); WILLIAM F. WHYTE, *Human Relations in the Restaurant Industry* (New York: McGraw-Hill Book Co., 1948); E. W. BAKKE, *Mutual Survival, The Goals of Unions and Managements* (New York: Harper Bros., 1946); ELIOT D. CHAPPLE, 'Applied Anthropology in Industry,' Chapter 45 in A. KROEBER, ed., *Anthropology Today* (Chicago: University of Chicago Press, 1953); TALCOTT PARSONS, *The Social System* (Cambridge: Harvard University Press, 1951); ROBERT K. MERTON, *Social Theory and Social Structure* (Glencoe: Free Press, 1949); and GEORGE HOMANS, *The Human Group* (New York: Harcourt, Brace & Co., 1951).

out its friction-generating points, could be explained, in part, by French feelings that France had restored her autonomy and initiative and had found the first of a series of ways to resist complete integration into the larger systems. If there was not a fusion of goals, the independent action of France bared forth a realization, on both sides, of the interdependence of the two nations inside a larger network.[22] The return of Charles de Gaulle to power in 1958 contributed to a more stable means of keeping French autonomy and opening channels for two-way communication.[23]

Looking at the French case again from the perspective of leadership studies in industrial plant sociology, let us focus on Arensberg's and Tootell's phrasing of earlier research by Lewin, Simon, Shartle, Guetzkow, and Argyris on permissive leaders and participation.

. . . this body of cases confirms existing discoveries that the leadership which sets off our process (interaction) is that which somehow combines coordination toward common goals with receptivity toward, even stimulation of, initiative from among the led.[24]

In an interview in Paris, April 3, 1960, B. said:

Khrushchev has come to see de Gaulle as Eisenhower did . . . With Dulles dead and MacMillan having his troubles with the Soviets, we are now in a position to help the whole West by showing the Russians that we can take the lead for

22. See EDGAR J. FURNISS, *France: Keystone of Western Defense* (Garden City: Doubleday & Co., 1954), pp. XVII + 77. This is not intended to overlook the satisfactions accorded to Britain for performance in the same events at Suez. France, Britain, and Israel, by acting independently and taking the initiative by avoiding the United States, established thereby an autonomous grouping within the Atlantic nations, providing an arrangement Lévi-Strauss has said 'may serve to prevent or control failures in functional reciprocity.' Lévi-Strauss, 'Social Structure,' in KROEBER *et al.*, eds., *Anthropology Today* (Chicago: Chicago University Press, 1953) describes such a mutual sharing of structures by the paradigm: A supplies B's needs, B supplies C's, and C supplies A's.

23. Through their identification with de Gaulle's speaking, initiating actions, providing ideas and suggestions, and attracting consultation by President Eisenhower (e.g., the Eisenhower trip made to Paris before the Khrushchev visit to the United States), French individuals like B. could feel that they had a way of transferring their feelings of indebtedness to a chief of state who could liquidate them by offering the intangible national gifts of advice and consent. De Gaulle, moreover, provided further psychological alternatives to countergifts when, in April 1960, he invited Khrushchev on a state visit to France, thus initiating actions with persons outside the Atlantic alliance who were in a deposition to do harm to the American donor-teachers. Identification with de Gaulle as the chief actor in the national search for reciprocity was enhanced by the power of mass communications.

24. CONRAD ARENSBERG and GEOFFREY TOOTELL, 'Plant Sociology: Real Discoveries and New Problems,' in MIRRA KOMAROVSKY, ed., *Common Frontiers of the Social Sciences* (Glencoe: Free Press, 1957), pp. 324-325.

a change, and that Western Europe is not a collection of satellites. What is interesting, too, is that even the Communists know that they have to consult each other; Khrushchev spends as much time in Budapest and Prague, it seems, as he spends in Moscow ... Dulles and Eisenhower did not pay us that much attention before; but now things are different.

B. was not saying that the United States had stimulated France to take the initiative, but that de Gaulle's initiative in matters that 'lesser men' (Frenchmen before de Gaulle) had left to the Americans now was being recognized by the Americans as a 'force to be dealt with.' The psychological effect was the same: morale had been improved from just the elements (productivity and initiative) which Lewin identified as contributing to morale in small groups.[25] The invitation by a donor nation to a receiver nation to give the donor advice (with this advice serving as a countergift) would produce similar consequences in morale.[26]

Arensberg and Tootell warn that 'the connections between experience in one institution and that in another are matters for objective study of societal functional integration ... not matters for hasty speculative extrapolation.'[27] Even with this precaution, fully aware that the shift of focus from carefully observed small groups to complex nations is full of methodological difficulties and dangers, I find that generalizations about the behavior of industrial workers are pertinent to an understanding of the behavior and attitudes of B. in the context of international technical assistance. Let us now compare his case with the experience of the Harwood Manufacturing Company at its pajama factory in Virginia. Quoted by Arensberg, the findings of Harwood industrial experiments, in varying amounts of participation by workers in decision-making, are described as follows:

The degree of morale ... (presumably satisfaction) was proportional to the degree of participation ... Aggressive criticism ... against management was highest in the non-participation group ... low in the representative ... no[ne] under total participation ... Turnover and absenteeism highest in the non-participation ... lowest in the total participation.[28]

25. KURT LEWIN in G. WATSON, ed., *Civilian Morale*, p. 56.
26. A summary of American views on consultation and participation as administrative techniques is found in WILTON S. DILLON, 'French Higher Education and the New Managerial Elite,' (typescript), 1957, p. 65.
27. CONRAD ARENSBERG and GEOFFREY TOOTELL, *op. cit.*, p. 328.
28. CONRAD M. ARENSBERG, 'Behavior and Organization: Industrial Studies,' in JOHN H. ROHRER and M. SHERIF, *Social Psychology at the Crossroads* (New York: Harper and Bros., 1951), p. 334. Arensberg adds: 'Leadership, supervision, participation in the process of making decisions are alike in that they are classes of events of interpersonal, interactive, social relationship ...,' *loc. cit.*

These findings could be paraphrased, in the language of Mauss' generalizations about gift exchange and applied to the French case,[29] as: The degree of morale was proportional to the degree of opportunity for the receiving nation to return gifts (participate . . .). Aggressive criticism against the donor nation (management) was highest among nations given the least opportunity to discharge their obligations (take part in decisions) by making countergifts . . . Absenteeism (or threat of it) from the alliance is less likely among those nations giving gifts (participation). . . . The donor nation (supervising manager) can reduce humiliation of the receiver nations by inviting them (workers) to take the initiative in making countergifts (consent, advice, and suggestions) . . . thus assuring an increase in morale and productivity through reciprocity (two-way communication).

Going back to the concrete basis of this study, I should point out again that my informant's morale seemed to increase in proportion to his feeling that he was giving back political knowledge (French know-how in dealing with Moslems) in exchange for the American idea of productivity. A system of defining equivalence in values of such intangible commodities did not exist.[30] The absence of bookkeeping devices, however, could not

29. The Franco-American strains in the Atlantic alliance can also be understood through generalizations made from another study of small group behavior. William F. Whyte's *Street Corner Society* analyzing leadership and control in the social structure of a corner gang in Chicago, gives another clue to the importance of communication and leadership in establishing feelings of reciprocity among group members. Homans, George, in *The Human Group* (New York: Harcourt, Brace & Co., 1951) gives White's study as an example of how reciprocity acts as a form of social control: 'Let us choose a norm that is one of the world's commonest: if a man does a favor for you, you must do a roughly equivalent favor for him in return. Unlike economists, we do not need to go into the question of what constitutes equivalence or price – how many yams are worth a fish in one society, how many votes are worth a job in another. Equivalence varies from favor to favor and group to group,' pp. 284-285.

Mauss no doubt would recognize as further evidence of his search for a human universal Whyte's description: 'The code of the corner boy requires him to help his friends when he can and to refrain from doing anything to harm them. When life in the group runs smoothly, the obligations binding members to one another are not explicitly recognized. . . . It's only when the relationship breaks down that the underlying obligations are brought to light . . .' *ibid.*, p. 285. Whyte, in the original work, makes another point relevant to understanding larger human groupings like the Atlantic alliance: '. . . A system of mutual obligations . . . is fundamental to group cohesion,' p. 256.

30. In the Buin district of Bougaineville, a debtor, when he returns small money, adds anything from 10 to 15 percent, or else gives the creditor a pig. Other examples of how a primitive society has worked out a more exact (than the Marshall Plan) exchange system, by classifying equivalences, are found in: DOUGLAS OLIVER, *A Solomon Island Society* (Cambridge, Mass.: Harvard University Press, 1955), p. 307, and CYRIL S. BELSHAW, *In Search of Wealth*, American Anthropological Association

remove the psychological force which, as Mauss said, 'compels the recipient to make a return.'[31] Included in the flow of messages being forced 'up the line' to American donors were meanings, detected through voice tone and gesture,[32] which I paraphrase and interpret as follows: 'You Americans have not consulted us (about our North African experience, science, or technology). Therefore, we will not consult you (in moments like Suez) when we know better than you what is best for the Western world (in showing force, with or without U.S. atomic help, because Moslems respect strength and authority). It is our obligation to show the way, and we do not expect you necessarily to be grateful to us until history proves us correct.'

The foregoing brief extrapolation from industrial studies suggests that communication and leadership can be useful in analyzing disturbances between donors and receivers in an international alliance. Until a more systematic search can be made for analogues of structure and process in the organization of a factory or a vast military and technical assistance program, the following proposition may suffice: *Consultation, as a part of the communication process, can serve as a gift-returning mechanism in human groups where knowledge and intellectual services are valued as exchange commodities. When the donor-teacher invites (leads) the pupil-receiver to participate in decisions that are likely to affect both parties, the latter is less likely to seek other alternatives to remove his obligations. Indeed, the receiver-pupil may consider that his advice and consultation constitutes a countergift.*[33]

Memoir No. 80, February 1955. (See especially Belshaw's discussion of reciprocity and marriage exchanges in Chapter 4, pp. 21-31.) Pacific societies found equivalences for tangible commodities. In the North Atlantic, with knowledge serving as a gift, the receiver had no system of repaying knowledge with knowledge. However, the chances for eventually working out systematic exchanges were enhanced by the U.S.S.R.'s sputnik challenge to the American patrimony of scientific and industrial knowledge in 1958. The U.S. became increasingly sensitive to the value of knowledge held by anyone, particularly persons and nations within the same exchange area, and more formal arrangements were made to collect, through explicit exchange or purchase, inventions, discoveries, and research of others. Thus both primitive and industrial societies, with tangible and intangible gifts, reflect Mauss' statement that 'A gift necessarily implies the notion of credit.' (M. MAUSS, *The Gift*, p. 55.)

31. *Ibid.*, p. 1.

32. Cf. EDWARD T. HALL, Jr., *The Silent Language* (Garden City: Doubleday & Co., 1959).

33. This proposition grows out of several sources. First, I am indebted to Prof. Solon T. Kimball for his discussions of consultation as an administrative and community process which helps innovators overcome resistance to change. Cf. S. T. KIMBALL and M. PEARSALL, *Talladega Story* (University: University of Alabama Press, 1954), xxxii + 259 pp. Also, I have found useful Prof. Conrad Arensberg's sug-

If perspectives from industrial groups help us to see more clearly the kinds of structures and communication processes conductive to handling the obligations of giving, receiving, and repaying, we will obtain similar rewards through a brief look at the Melanesian institution of gift exchange called the *kula* ring.[34] As described by Malinowski and interpreted by Mauss, the *kula* is an overseas trading voyage linking the Massim area of the Pacific in a vast complex institution of ritual exchange.[35]

---

gestion that I read PETER BLAU, *The Dynamics of Bureaucracy* (Chicago: University Chicago Press, 1955), in which I found these relevant clues to intellectual services and consultation as gifts in a technical assistance situation: 'Peer relationships rest on reciprocity in social exchange. Unilateral services engender obligations which destroy equality of status and erect barriers to the free flow of communication ... (p. 204). Social cohesion depends on basic equality of status. Co-operative interaction, such as the pattern of consultation, therefore affects it in two opposite ways. Co-operation is a major source of cohesion in work groups, because it unites members in the voluntary exchange of valued assistance, but it simultaneously weakens cohesion by giving rise of status distinctions which inhibit social intercourse and thus limit feelings of fellowship. . . .,

'A consultation can be considered an exchange of values; both participants gain something, and both have to pay a price. The questioning agent is enabled to perform better than he could otherwise have done, without exposing his difficulties to the supervisor. By asking for advice, he implicitly pays his respect to the superior proficiency of his colleague. *This acknowledgement of inferiority is the cost of receiving assistance* [italics mine]. The consultant gains prestige, in return for which he is willing to devote some time to the consultation and permit it to disrupt his own work (p. 108). The recognition of both participants in a consultation that one provided an *intellectual service* [italics mine] to the other raised the status of the consultant and sub-ordinated or obligated the questioner to him. These were the inducements for the consultant to give advice and, simultaneously, the cost incurred by the questioner for receiving it ... In the absence of an awareness that a service was furnished, no need existed for the speaker to reciprocate for the help he did, in fact, obtain. He did not subordinate or obligate himself to listeners.' (p. 109.)

34. Cf. *Argonauts of the Western Pacific: An Account of Native Enterprise and Adventure in the Archipelagoes of Melanesian New Guinea* (New York: E. P. Dutton, 1953), esp. Ch. III, 'Essentials of the Kula,' pp. 81-104. In comparing exchange practices of pre-literate men of the South Pacific and industrial men of the North Atlantic, I have found a pertinent observation by Herskovits: 'The distinctions between literate and non-literate economies are those of degree rather than kind.' Cf. M. HERSKOVITS, *Economic Anthropology* (New York: Knopf, 1952), p. 488.

35. Borrowing on C. G. Seligman's earlier study of South Sea trade routes (*Melanesians of British New Guinea*, Cambridge, 1910), Malinowski expanded his focus of attention from the Southern Massim to an area embracing the Louisiades, Woodlark Island, the Trobriand archipelago, and the d'Entrecasteaux group, following the indirect effects of the trading system to such outlying districts as Rossel island and some parts of the Northern and Southern coast of New Guinea.

Mauss called it 'a kind of grand potlatch.'[36] Oliver has described it as 'an elaborate peace-keeping mechanism.'[37] The principal significance of the *kula* for sharpening our understanding North Atlantic exchanges lies in its safety-value and gift-returning mechanisms which are so well built into the exchange systems that everybody has a chance to be a donor and to maintain his dignity. The receiver, while temporarily possessing the gift, knows that he has a way to make a return gift. He has a real hope of discharging his obligation. He has the pleasure of being a donor and reciprocating. His gift behavior is so prescribed by custom[38] that he knows what is expected of him. This was not the case with B., who had to improvise ways to return to a donor-teacher role and reciprocate. In the *kula* ring, the roles of donor and receiver are reversed at appropriate intervals.

What is exchanged in the *kula* ring? How does it work?

While B. travelled in quest of knowledge, the participants in the *kula* ring travel to give and receive tangibles: red shell necklaces (soulava) and white-shelled bracelets (swali).[39] The objects caught up in the ring circulate constantly. Their circulation performs various functions. As we read Malinowski's description of the counter-clockwise and clockwise flow of gifts, let us keep in mind Mauss' comparison of the *kula* with the potlatch: *both institutions involve giving and receiving, the donors on one occasion being the recipients on the next.*[40] Malinowski wrote:

36. M. MAUSS, *The Gift*, p. 20.
37. DOUGLAS OLIVER, *The Pacific Islands* (Cambridge: Harvard University Press, 1952), p. 40.
38. Cf. B. MALINOWSKI, *Crime and Custom in Savage Society* (New York: The Humanities Press, 1951), esp. Ch. VIII, 'The Principle of Give and Take Pervading Tribal Life,' pp. 39-45.
39. With B.'s voyage, we have some reminders of Malinowski's description of 'The Departure of an Overseas Expedition,' an account of a *kula* voyage from Sinaketa to Dobu. Cf. *Argonauts of the Western Pacific: An Account of Native Enterprise and Adventure in the Archipelagoes of Melanesian New Guinea* (New York: E. P. Dutton, 1953), p. 195. French households, regardless of the different social grades of members of the mission, were alike, as were those in Sinaketa, in being astir with activity before the departure. Wives made gifts of tinned foods (*paté, escargots*) for their husbands to take on the voyage; there was a great deal of joking about the husbands being unable to survive the hardships of being away from French cooking for their six weeks in America. Late hours were kept talking about and preparing for the journey. Travelling in a plane rather than a canoe, B. sought industrial know-how rather than material objects. But like the *kula* participants, he came home with necklaces and bracelets, products of mass production, purchased as souvenirs at Times Square in New York. In his dealings, as chief of mission, with the American donors, B.'s only rituals were the speeches of thanks he offered after factory visits, banquets and cocktail parties.
40. *The Gift*, p. 20.

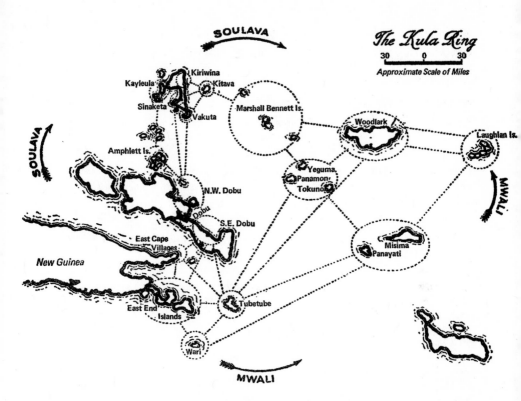

The Kula Ring

SOULAVA

30   0   30
Approximate Scale of Miles

Kayleula
Kiriwina
Kitava
Sinaketa
Vakuta
Marshall Bennett Is.
Woodlark
Laughlan Is.
SOULAVA
Amphlett Is.
N.W. Dobu
Dobu
Yeguma,
Panamon,
Tokuno
MWALI
S.E. Dobu
East Cape
Villages
Misima
Panayati
New Guinea
East End
Islands
Tubetube
Wari
MWALI

Each of these articles, as it travels in its own direction on the closed circuit, meets on its way articles of the other class, and is constantly being exchanged for them. Every movement of the Kula articles, every detail of the transactions is fixed and regulated by a set of traditional rules and conventions, and some acts of the Kula are accompanied by an elaborate magical ritual and public ceremonies . . . One transaction does not finish the Kula relationship, the rule being 'once in the Kula, always in the Kula,' and a partnership between two men is a permanent and lifelong affair.[41]

The building of seagoing canoes for expeditions, preparatory taboos, ordinary trade (*gimwali*), and certain forms of mortuary ceremonies are types of activity that take place before the *kula* or are associated with it. 'The Kula,' Malinowski continued, 'is thus an extremely big and complex institution. . . It welds together a considerable number of tribes, and it embraces a fast complex of activities, inter-connected, and playing into one another, so as to form one organic whole.'[42]

These accounts of the workings and functions of the *kula* help to point up the psychological advantage its participants seem to enjoy in contrast

41. *Argonauts of the Western Pacific*, pp. 82-83.
42. In analyzing the Marshall Plan and the Atlantic Alliance as a system of gift

to persons we have seen caught up in the Marshall Plan 'ring' where certain blockages (e.g., non-matching notions of reciprocal behavior) impede the free flow of intellectual and other goods from receivers back to donors. What are at least two conditions leading to such psychological advantages for the *kula* men? One is the feeling of autonomy and independence when a *kula* participant both gives and receives. The other is the feeling of interdependence when one recognizes he is part of a larger universe. The latter feelings grow out of a division of labor[43] which represents the various products, talents, and skills of culturally diverse groups making up the *kula* system. Mauss saw the advantages of autonomy and independence when he analyzed *kula* reciprocities:

Pains are taken to show one's freedom and autonomy as well as one's magnanimity, yet all the time one is animated by the mechanisms of obligation ... resident in the gifts themselves.[44]

---

exchange, it is important to remember the distinctions between the way an ethnographer views or interprets reality, and the way reality is seen by the subject or informant. Malinowski, for example, in presenting the essentials of the *kula*, remarked: '... What appears to us an extensive, complicated and yet well ordered institution is the outcome of ever so many doings and pursuits, carried on by savages, who have no laws or aims or charters definitely laid down. They know their own motives, know the purpose of individual actions and the rules which apply to them, but how, out of these, the whole collective institution shapes, this is beyond their mental range. Not even the most intelligent native has any clear idea of the Kula as a big, organized social construction, still less of its sociological function and implications ... The integral picture does not exist in his mind ... The ethnographer has to *construct* the picture of the big institution, very much as the physicist constructs his theory from the experimental data which always have been within the reach of everybody, but which needed a consistent interpretation.' (*Ibid.*, pp. 83-84.) While dealing with such complex entities as nations within industrial civilization, the *kula* model may seem quite far-fetched to persons unaccustomed to looking for human universals. Malinowski, however, seems to have anticipated such inquiries as this one when he wrote: '... The Kula, if it represents a novel, but not freakish, indeed, a fundamental type of human activity and of mental attitude of man, we may expect to find allied and kindred phenomena in various other ethnographic provinces ... It would be futile ... to expect exact replicas of this institution ... What we can expect to find in other parts of the world are the fundamental ideas of the Kula, and its social arrangements in their main outline, and for these the field worker might be on the lookout.' (*Ibid.*, pp. 514-515.)
43. Cf. EMILE DURKHEIM, *The Division of Labor in Society*, G. Simpson, transl., 3rd printing (Glencoe: Free Press, 1949). Durkheim analysed the work of Herbert Spencer: 'Spencer says that each man can maintain himself through his work, can exchange his produce for the goods of another, can lend assistance and receive payment, can enter into some association for pursuing some enterprise, small or large, without obeying the direction of society in its totality ... Under these conditions, only the remaining link between men would be that of an absolutely free exchange.' (p. 200.)
44. *The Gift*, p. 2.

The persons participating in *kula* exchanges seem to find their freedom and autonomy by the leeway permitted in the system to keep articles for unspecified periods of time.[45] The possessor has the free choice, the chance to decide when he shall relinquish the gift and present it to the next person or group. Of course, the momentum of the system, activated by obligations, brings restraints and controls, but these apparently do not outweigh the rewards felt by individuals in participating in a larger whole.

While autonomy and control of obligations are thus served by the chance to exercise choice in the timing of offering gifts, a related advantage is the opportunity for people in the diverse cultures in the system to keep their separate identities. Fortune, in *Sorcerers of Dobu*, for example, suggests the diversity possible within the system:

To the native, the giving to him of a most valuable present by a man of a strange place, the giving of such extensive credit, such reliance placed on his commercial honesty, is an annually repeated miracle ... Knowing also of Dobuan distrust of, and lack of hospitality to strangers, his fear of strange sorcery, the fact that he is given hospitality and fed by his host, his *kula* partner abroad, may well be viewed, as he views it, as one of the strange miracles of magic.[46]

Providing such pleasant surprises to the Dobuans, with their differing landscape and character, is only one of the attractions of the *kula* for the various participants. All are drawn together by the anticipation of receiving and later giving the two main *kula* articles, the arm shells and shell strings. These are primarily ornaments which have no more practical use than, as Malinowski suggested, the Crown jewels in Edinburgh Castle.[47] However, the movement of these objects exposes a division of labor. While the ceremonial objects move, satisfying prestige and sociability of participants,

45. *Argonauts of the Western Pacific*, p. 95.
46. Cf. REO F. FORTUNE, *Sorcerers of Dobu* (London: Routledge & Sons, Ltd., 1932), p. 215. Malinowski, writing a preface to this volume, contrasted the Dobuans with the Trobrianders: 'There seem to be typical differences which run through the two cultures: the Trobriand system is more elaborate, more methodical, containing more well-thought-out details and logical schemes.' Ruth Benedict, also noting the cultural contrasts in the *kula*, wrote of the Dobuans in *Patterns of Culture* (New York: Mentor Books, 1934): 'The passion for endless reciprocal commercial transactions that grips so much of Melanesia is present also in Dobu,' she states in introducing the point that suspicion and treachery do not inhibit Dobuans from entering into reciprocal relationships with others who may have quite different economic circumstances and motives which help define success and place value on the accumulation of goods (p. 120). Mauss also took note of how Trobriand culture was projected from its home base and accommodated matching elements from other cultures represented in the ring. He spoke of an 'internal *kula*' and an 'external *kula*.' (M. MAUSS, *The Gift*, pp. 26-27.)
47. *Argonauts of the Western Pacific*, p. 88.

they also make possible a straightforward exchange of useful goods (*gimwali*). The interdependence based on local specialization of industries is secondary to the ceremonial aspects of the ring. But the human contacts thus established leads to the discovery that some people polish greenstone, another group makes canoes, another carves wood, and still another mixes paint.

What do these *kula* characteristics help us to understand about contrasts in the type of gift relationships between nations in the North Atlantic alliance? Both the *kula* ring and the Marshall Plan represent: a) supra-societal arrangements which bind a variety of racial, language, and cultural groups into a web of transactions; and b) a potential division of labor among the human aggregations involved. However, the *kula* provides a striking difference with its stable and predictable exchanges between people who reverse their donor and receiver roles. The Marshall Plan did not represent such an exchange. The chance for a receiver to reciprocate with a gift to which he attached value had not been built into the system. Without such a balancing mechanism, recipients felt obliged to invent their own ways of returning gifts and forcing them upon the donor. Nevertheless, the Marshall Plan, seen as a system of *potential* gift exchange, contained nascent elements which bore functional resemblances to the *kula*. For example, knowledge, if handled as a primary commodity in the transactions of literate, industrial nations, compares with the ceremonial and practical commodities exchanged by pre-literate groups within the *kula*. Tangible objects of the *kula* participants reflect an inter-tribal division of labor just as intangible gifts of knowledge might reveal intellectual specialization and sharing on the part of modern countries. National societies may have different intellectual products and emphases (technological, scientific, literary). Different types of knowledge, for literate societies, may be as useful for distinguishing certain people as are the polished greenstone, canoes, or pottery for the people of Melanesia or Papua.[48] The significant difference lies in the supra-societal handling of obligations growing out of the circulation of goods. As we have already seen, *kula*-type reciprocity was absent in the Atlantic alliance. So long as the biggest, youngest nation was unaware of the obligations felt by smaller, older nations to repay what

48. I heard the late William Faulkner, the American novelist, draw applause in Paris in July 1952 when he said to an international audience of Europeans: 'We (Americans) are the muscle, and you (Europeans) are the brain; we must work together.' French businessmen I interviewed often referred to the technological genius of the United States, keeping to France the speciality of arts and letters and theoretical science, leaving to 'lesser persons' the problem of applying theories for military or industrial uses. Similarly, Japanese have gone to Germany to study engineering and medicine and to France for literature, mathematics, and philosophy.

they consider to be debts, the alliance ran the risk of cleavages and conficts which could have resulted in temporary disruptions to the 'organic whole.'[49]

An assumption held through all the foregoing discussion of the demands for reciprocity – as they operate among industrial workers, street gangs, or members of productivity teams receiving foreign aid – is that the *kula* ring has heuristic value for understanding or designing transactions which occur within international systems of technical assistance.

In the concluding chapter, some of the implications of this study will be explored.

D. SUMMARY

This chapter has been an effort to show how reciprocity or, in its absence, a set of compensating mechanisms, is a necessary condition for: a) the control of hostility growing out of unfulfilled obligations; b) a source of self-esteem, autonomy, initiative, and morale for individuals, groups, or nations suffering from a loss of status through frustrated discharge of felt obligations; and c) maintaining group cohesion.

The 'compensating mechanisms' discussed here have included: a) a receiver's going outside the original interaction system with the donor to escape supervision and patronage, thereby calling attention to his desire to give as well as to receive; b) creating channels of communication by initiating messages 'up the line' to the donor (letters, pamphlets, mass media, diplomatic consultation), thus establishing psychological alternatives to countergifts; and c) consolidating these mechanisms with technological and political power sufficient to load, initiate, and give, thereby creating the degree of autonomy necessary to continue, 'with honor,' participation in a larger network of interactions, obligations, and inter-dependences which make up groups, coalitions, or alliances.

49. Cf. François Pérroux's discussion of the asymmetrical relations between the old and young nations that make up the 'Euratlantic orbit,' in his book, *L'Europe sans rivages* (Paris: Presses Universitaires de France, 1954), pp. 85-163.

CHAPTER V

CONCLUSION: THE OBLIGATION TO SPECULATE AND INQUIRE

The central objective of this study has been to seek greater universality for the ideas of Marcel Mauss related to gift exchange. In pushing his generalizations to a larger universe, the contemporary world where industrial men give and try to pay back donors with both things and knowledge, I have encountered a new obligation: to speculate and inquire about the implications of this study for moral discourse, future research, and public policy. First, however, the question asked in the opening paragraph of the introduction must be given pointed and critical attention. Do Mauss' generalizations about exchange relationships among pre-literate and ancient men apply to people who live in modern industrial societies? In giving an affirmative answer, I wish to make four qualifications.[1] They are:

1) Despite the minute attention Mauss gave to the analysis of other scholars' ethnographic data, his theory of obligation is useful primarily because of its 'coarse-grain' nature. *Les trois obligations: donner, recevoir,*

---

1. These are intended to show that I have the benefit of hindsight and the results of new research on human behavior and international relations to which Mauss did not have access during his lifetime. My understanding of one of the canons of scholarship is that truth-seeking requires critical judgment and the evaluation of older theories in the light of new concept and evidence. Seen in historical perspective, Mauss' generalizations about gifts and obligations survive magnificently the sophistication of modern behavioral research as well as empirical testing in the complex arena of international technical assistance. With his historical limitations in mind, and withholding a judgment that might reproach Mauss for not doing more than he intended in *The Gift*, I find my most critical reaction to Mauss a parallel to a critic of Robert K. Merton's typology of modes of individual adaptation: 'To be frank ... I find his typology too neat and too pat to ring true. But there just isn't any other generalized theory of deviant behavior around. The job he's done is so polished and stimulating that until something better comes along we'll all have to use it.' See MORTON M. HUNT, 'Profiles, How Does it Come to Be So?' *New Yorker*, January 28, 1961, p. 59. This profile of Professor Merton refers to a typology published in R. MERTON, *Social Theory and Social Structure* (Glencoe: Free Press, 1949), p. 133.

rendre[2] are beautiful in their simplicity, brevity, and inclusiveness. These very characteristics, however, carry with them a challenge for students of human behavior to be more specific than was Mauss about the structural, cultural, and situational contexts in which gifts influence the strains or balances in interpersonal relations. The insights to be gained by analyzing gift behavior in diverse societies, greatly separated in time and space and varying from the simple to the complex, are due to the abstract nature of Mauss' formula. Never losing sight of the concrete, Mauss nevertheless provides in his abstraction the vision of the whole, the interdependence of the three elements of the giving, receiving, and repaying process. Mauss' schema thus helps us to cast a wide, magnetic net. He leaves to others the task of sorting out and accounting for the various items in the catch: the variables of class, region, age, occupation, sex, status, and religion as they affect the ebb and flow of gifts.

2) Mauss gave little if any explicit attention to gift behavior involving persons of different national cultures. The transaction to which he gave his major attention were intra-tribal (Kwakiutl potlatch), intra-caste (classical Brahmin), or intra-societal (ancient Roman). For the purpose of this study, his analysis of such supra-societal exchanges as the *kula* was, at best, heuristic. His interpretation of the *kula* showed that people of differing traditions could organize reciprocity in their gift institutions and that cultural differences need not impede exchange. So Mauss prepared the way, but students from this and later generations are left to find out if his generalizations continue to fit the evidence from international and cross-cultural gift situations involving industrial nations.

3) In view of the increased complexity of industrial societies and the specialized knowledge needed to help make them function, knowledge can be analyzed as a commodity. Mauss asserted that 'everything is stuff to be given away and repaid.' He did not demonstrate, however, either with an empirical or a hypothetical case, the possibility of treating knowledge like tangible goods. This study, therefore, has had to go beyond Mauss' materials to propose that: the giving, receiving, and repaying process involving knowledge as a gift is not unlike the process of handling beads, pottery, food, or other tangibles which circulate among people and become a part of their networks of building up and discharging obligations. A related post-Mauss proposition is that knowledge can become a potential countergift. That is, if knowledge (e.g., about technology and human organization) is offered as a gift, the recipient has a chance to make a countergift in kind. Once possessed by the recipient for sufficient time to

2. This essence of Mauss' essay on gifts has been stated by Lévi-Strauss in his introduction to the works of Mauss, *Sociologie et Anthropologie* (Paris: Presses Universitaires de France, 1950), p. xxxviii.

be endowed with the marks of his own intellectual tradition, knowledge becomes something new. Intellectual goods are subject to synthesis and re-classification and may take on new value to the donor when offered back, so to speak, in a new package for further circulation.[3]

4) Another hiatus in Mauss' works, for the purpose of this study, is the absence of a conceptual framework for describing and analyzing the strains and compensatory mechanisms which seem present when donors and recipients lack an institutionalized means of discharging obligations toward each other. The sources of frustrated gift behavior are implied by Mauss in his discussion of humiliation and dignity as potential elements in gift situations. Refinements on the obligation to repay are needed, however, to account for symbolic and psychological substitutes for countergifts.[4]

With these qualifications in mind, can it still be said that Mauss' theory of obligation is adequate? Is his conceptualization of gift processes suitable for understanding the obligations felt by industrial men as well as pre-literate and ancient men who received gifts? Through this and other efforts to extend Mauss' ideas to a complex universe beyond his data, will behavioral scientists be in a better position to predict the conditions which may create strains or maintain equilibrium in international donor-recipient relationships? This case study leads me once again to say yes to these questions about the universality and durability of *Essai sur le don*. Mauss has provided the basis for a hypothesis about a social process which seems to offer an explanation of a great number of phenomena. Adequate testing is yet to come. Thus, this study should be considered exploratory, a part of the discovery of the variables out of which more precise hypotheses and research methods can be developed.[5] In the meantime, the evidence so far

3. From a historical perspective, the potential French countergift to the Americans represented by French 'improvements' on the American phrasing and presentation of the idea of productivity is but one contemporary instance of a larger case of intellectual reciprocity. For example, the Arabic gift of Greek thought (Ptolemy's astronomy and Aristotle's *Physics*) given back to the Western world after having been nurtured by the Arabs since Hellenism; and the pre-revolutionary Chinese going to Japan to receive the Japanese improvements on original Chinese ideographs, the Japanese having made a linguistic countergift of inventing accessory characters needed to convey modern science and technology. These are intellectual analogues to gifts of wine or cheese which might be offered and then returned with increased value after protection, aging, and tasting.

4. Such as the compensatory or safety-valve mechanisms, already mentioned in this study, which were symptoms of a quest for reciprocity, self-esteem, autonomy and initiative on the part of persons who felt themselves objects of one-way, downward giving.

5. The case of B., for example, represents a summary of variables, all interconnected, any one of which could be studied quantitatively through sampling procedures developed by specialists in survey design and analysis. Thus B., by participating in an

at hand points to a human condition which I find at the base of much that is going on in the world of foreign aid and technological and social change and, above all, the world where people, affected by these processes, are searching for reciprocity and the dignity of donorship. Let us speculate, then, on some of the implications of this study for moral discourse and for future research and public policy. These concluding paragraphs will refer to both the 'ought' and 'is' of gifts.

A. THEOLOGY AND MORALS

'Another theme plays its part in the economy and morality of the gift: that of the gift made to man in the sight of gods or nature,'[6] Mauss wrote in recognizing the interplay of gifts and religion in human life. The gifts offered and received by industrial men are also made in the sight of gods or nature. (See Chapter II.) Theologians and moralists, therefore, might well turn their attention to the following questions if they are interested in giving new interpretations of God-man and man-man relationships in the light of contemporary world politics and social science.[7] 1) Should Christian concepts of grace and charity, pain and suffering, mercy and justice, embrace the idea that man may be close to the divine model of compassion when he understands the pain of carrying obligation and thus provides persons with a healing release from obligation? That is, what truth is there in the paradox: while Christian mercy exalts the free gift, Christian mercy may be found in the man who releases his debtors from obligation by asking for return gifts? 2) Are there new ways for donor nations or individuals to forgive debts than rather pretending debts do not exist?

---

international alliance as a carrier of knowledge of new technology and management techniques, is calling into play his other roles which link: a) family; b) a factory; c) a social class; and d) one nation and its relations with another nation. Cf. E. CHAPPLE and C. COON, *Principles of Anthropology*, who wrote: 'The reasons for the interdependence of institutions are very simple. Institutions do not exist in a vacuum; they are made up of individuals who, in complex society, are at the same time members of other institutions.' (P. 443.) See also the authors' discussions (p. 523) of the tribe, confederation and nation as 'maximum extension of the family' as a basis for making hypotheses and building research models.

6. *The Gift*, p. 12.

7. For a brief historical view of some of the great issues, raised by early Christian theologians, which have undergone new interpretations with scientific studies of man in the modern world, see R. FREEMAN BUTTS, 'The Ideas Men Lived By,' in his *A Cultural History of Education* (New York and London: McGraw-Hill Co., 1947), pp. 97-114. His reference to the idea of spiritual grace is the pertinent point of departure for a new theological view of free gifts and unfree gifts as they are offered and received by rich nations and poor nations.

3) How can weak and meek nations help strong and prideful nations find the grace to accept their gifts? 4) How does the seeking of gifts from the indebted reflect the traditional Christian concern for the primacy of the person and the use of talent?[8]

Such questions are only a few which are stimulated not only by Mauss' theory of obligation, but also by the intimate view of the human condition of B. and other recipients of technical assistance in the modern world. Perhaps an agenda for conferences of the Institute of Religious and Social Studies[9] might include a dialogue of psychiatrists, theologians, and anthropologists discussing: 'New Directions for Foreign Aid: Some Religious and Scientific Views on Gifts and Obligation.'

In Mauss' own discussion of the moral implications of his study of gifts, he wrote:

Society . . . seeks the individual in a curious frame of mind in which the sentiments of its own laws are mingled with other, purer sentiments: charity, social service and solidarity. The theme of the gift, of freedom and obligation in the gift, of generosity and self-interest in giving, reappear in our own society like the resurrection of a dominant motif long forgotten . . . *But a mere statement of what is taking place is not enough. We should deduce from it some course of action or moral precept.*[10] [italics mine] . . . Concrete study leads not only to a science of manners, a partial social science, but even to ethical conclusions – 'civility' or 'civics' . . .[11]

Mauss thus challenged the student of human behavior as well as the theologian and moralist. At the same time, he urged statesmen and citizens to plan and choose their actions on the basis of the findings of science and directions of moralists. Without saying that science and morals use the

8. These questions are partly inspired by conversations with Canon John Pyle, Cathedral of St. John the Divine, New York: Dr. Daisetz Suzuki, the Zen Buddhist philosopher, Kita-Kamakura, Japan; and the Rev. John N. Krumm, St. Paul's Chapel, Columbia University; and lectures by Dr. Reinhold Niebuhr and Dr. Paul Tillich, formerly of Union Theological Seminary, New York. Cf. also LEWIS MUMFORD, *The Condition of Man* (New York: Harcourt, Brace & Co., 1944), especially Ch. II, 'The Primacy of the Person,' pp. 51-75.

9. Cf. previous publications of the Religion and Civilization Series, Institute of Religious and Social Studies, a graduate school at the Jewish Theological Seminary of America, New York City, conducted in cooperation with Catholic, Jewish, and Protestant scholars. Also pertinent to such a conference would be a paper by Dr. Robert O. Carlson, sociologist, Standard Oil Company of New Jersey, 'Image and Polity: The Western Corporation and the Christian Church in an Overseas Setting' (in process). Dr. Carlson deals with the assumptions of reciprocity behind the expectation of various publics that these two institutions have 'a social responsibility' or obligation beyond selling oil or religion.

10. *The Gift*, p. 66.

11. *Ibid.*, p. 81.

same methods or lead necessarily to the same conclusions or imperatives, Mauss, I suspect, would have little trouble accepting the phrase: 'It is both good science and good morals' if applied to his actual appeal for persons, families, clans, tribes, and nations to initiate a 'rythm of communal and private labor, in wealth amassed and redistributed,' thereby finding 'mutual respect and reciprocal generosity.'[12] He proposed research which would lead societies, their sub-groups and members, to 'stabilize their contracts to give, receive, and repay.'[13] Mauss' appeals are reminders of the first sentence of his essay calling the reader's attention to some of the lines of the Scandinavian epic, the *Edda*:

I have never found a man so generous and hospitable that he would not receive a present, nor one so liberal with his money that he would dislike a reward if he could get one ... That friendship lasts longest – if there is a chance of its being a success – in which friends both give and receive gifts ... A gift always looks for recompense ...[14]

Explaining that the *Edda* outlines his subject matter, Mauss went on to make a plea for modern societies to learn from the social inventions of the savages, and, with educating man's reason to oppose emotion, he believed that we could 'set up the will for peace against rash follies ...'[15] (and) ... substitute alliance, gift and commerce for war, isolation and stagnation.'

B. FUTURE RESEARCH ON HUMAN ORGANIZATION AND PUBLIC POLICY

Mauss staggers the sociological imagination with such a challenge. He leaves us with the obligations to find out, no less, how gifts relate to war and peace.[16] How can students of human behavior describe or predict the conditions for steady relationships between people interacting in such

12. *Ibid.*, p. 81.
13. *Ibid.*, p. 80.
14. *Ibid.*, p. xiv.
15. *The Gift*, p. 80. Mauss was referring here to an incident reported by Richard Thurnwald in *Samoa-Inseln* to show how quickly people can pass from a feast to battle. Buleau, a chief, made a remark which caused him to be killed by a man belonging to another chief (Bobal). Bobal's men then ran off with the women of the village, a favorite theme of Claude Lévi-Strauss' analyses of social structure in *Les Structures Elémentaires de la Parenté*.
16. Without a reference to Mauss or gifts, a recent mimeographed study by a psychologist deals with reciprocity as a necessary element in reducing tensions created by threats of nuclear warfare. See CHARLES E. OSGOOD, *Graduated Reciprocation in Tension-Reduction: A Key to Initiative in Foreign Policy* (Urbana: Institute of Communications Research, University of Illinois, 1960), 82 pp.

varied kinds of human organizations as families, tribes, factories, gangs, or international alliances?[17] Recalling that B. felt both rewarded and punished by his having been caught up in a large universe of give and take, I invite – in the spirit of Marcel Mauss and his successors who want to add knowledge and apply it to human affairs – a search for operational meanings for the following two propositions:

Leadership as a Form of Inviting Gifts

Leadership, practiced by individuals and nations, consists of discovering the means by which individuals or nations feel indebted, and after discovering their potential gifts, asking them to offer their gifts toward a common goal or the common good. Recognition of positions of leadership is found in the willingness of followers to accept what the donor-leader-teacher thinks are the proper gifts to offer to a joint enterprise.[18] The giving and use of such gifts constitutes a specialization or role differentiation within the group. Thus gift exchange can be a form of dividing labor and utilizing human potentials.

Functional Reciprocity and Human Organization

Recognizing that knowledge of human behavior can be applied to both peace

17. In predicting or describing conditions for keeping an equilibrium in human affairs, it is useful to consider historical precedents. For example, I am grateful to Donald J. Munro, University of Michigan, for his calling to my attention two peaceful periods of Asian history that can be linked to institutionalized gift exchange within the respective societies. In personal correspondence from Taiwan, November 10, 1960, he wrote of balances which scholars have described in China and Japan: 'Gifts in Asia are mentioned by Jacques Gernet in *Les Aspects économiques du Bouddhisme dans la société chinoise du Ve au Xe siècle* (Saigon: Publications de l'Ecole Française d'Extrême Orient, 1956). He develops a thesis therein that: 'The Buddhist theory of the expiatory gift productive of spiritual benefits was the source of the productive use of capital ...' This all ties in with the growth of commerce and industry. Robert Bellah's *Tokugawa Religion* (Glencoe: Free Press, 1958) focuses a good deal of attention on the giving of a gift and repayment by the recipient as being at the basis of much Japanese ethics. For example, the Sun-goddess gives her life to the people as a gift and they owe loyalty to the state (i.e., the emperor who is the embodiment of the Sun-goddess) as repayment of that gift. The same holds in all relationships, such as that in which the clerk owes the merchant honesty and loyalty in exchange for his position.'
18. For example, an analysis of international relations from the stand-point of Mauss' theory of obligation might well start afresh on studying German reactions to American efforts in 1960-61 to enlist West German's financial and educational contributions to less developed countries, helping thereby to reduce the outflow of American gold and to provide Americans with a 'return' on their Marshall Plan investments. Whether Germans saw themselves in a hierarchical or egalitarian relationship vis-à-vis the United States would provide one clue to understanding the Germans' initial reluctance to accept U.S. leadership, i.e., doing the American bidding to offer German gifts toward a joint Western enterprise. Cf. ROBERT LOWIE, *Toward Understanding Germany* (Chicago: Chicago University Press, 1954), esp. section 'Classes and Rank,' pp. 71-193.

and war, a major task for peace-loving anthropologists and political leaders is to invent designs of human organization based upon the principle of functional reciprocity. Such designs would take into account the need for well-balanced chains of reciprocal services. Hostility and tension would be like elements in the balancing process as there are always problems of allocation and coordination, of balance between the parts. The making of gifts and the delivery of return gifts would be among the ways of organizing an equilibrium and the building of a common culture.

The task of designing types of human organization which would build functional reciprocity into a system of technical assistance relationships might start with a review of the already existing theoretical and applied approaches to some aspects of the above propositions. The volume, *Small Groups*,[19] contains empirical studies of leadership bearing on understanding donor-recipient relationships in such supra-national organizations as the Colombo Plan, the North Atlantic Treaty Organization or the organizational arrangements of the Soviet Union vis-à-vis China and Eastern Europe. One question which needs to be examined by both scientists and statesmen concerned with foreign aid is: Are there greater chances for equilibrium through bilateral or multi-national organization of aid? Would a *kula*-type (circular reciprocity) system provide a workable model for the offering and receiving of gifts between nations?

As a summary of this study and also as a shorthand inventory of organizational models on which new research might start, I will represent schematically below three patterns of gift behavior. The first two are bilateral. The third is circular. The first model is an example of 'pure' reciprocity in which A gives to B, B accepts and gives something back to A. A rhythm is established. An uninterrupted straight line identifies the actor who initiates gifts and becomes a donor. The broken line represents the response of the recipient who makes a countergift.

The symbol (+) signifies a positive termination of a sequence in which the recipient becomes a donor by making a countergift to the person (or collectivity) who offered the gift originally. The plus sign also refers to the situation where the offering and acceptance of the countergift reduces the strain of obligation for both parties; equilibrium is restored and the actors are ready for new interaction through gifts. The process is the same whether the gifts are tangible or intangible. The point in the schematic where the plus sign appears is an abstraction of Mauss' prescription for balanced relationships: 'Both give and receive, the donors on one occasion being the recipients on the next.'

In contrast, the minus symbol (—) refers to situations where the recipi-

19. See P. HARE, E. BORGATTA and R. BALES, eds., *Small Groups* (New York: Alfred A. Knopf, 1955).

ent is deprived of his chance to reverse his role and become a donor. The donor continues to initiate gifts without a provision for the recipient to handle obligations with honor. This may vary with different structural and cultural contexts. Whether hierarchical or egalitarian relationships are involved or whether an exact system of equivalences of gifts has been worked out, the deprivation of recipients of their chances to give something back is the meaning I attach here to Mauss' statement: 'Failure to make return gifts means a loss of dignity.'

Next in the schematic is a combination of plus and minus signs ($\pm$). I use these to refer to situations which here will be called 'pseudo reciprocity,' i.e., the prevailing gift arrangements which are rejected by the recipient at the same time the donor, innocent of the recipient's feelings, continues to offer gifts. In such a situation, the recipient tries to reverse the flow of downward giving by substituting countergifts to which he attaches value (advice, criticism, cultural or intellectual services). The more insistent the donor seems in refusing to recognize the recipient's desire for reciprocity, the greater the recipient's latent desire to force a gift 'up the line' toward the donor. This place in the schematic thus sums up a proposition which I have phrased tentatively as follows: 'Whether through indifference, innocence or a conscious effort to preserve status by refusing to accept gifts, the donor . . . incurs the hostility of the receiver . . . to the extent that the donor frustrates the discharge of . . . felt obligation.'

Finally, the symbol ($\times$) refers to situations in which the recipient tries to cancel his obligation, by now a demoralizing burden, by forcing the donor to recognize his ability to give and initiate. By now, the recipient has taken matters into his own hands. The latent desire to give has become manifest. Lacking the social arrangements to make countergifts, he presses gifts upon the donor. He takes independent action without supervision from the donor. He offers advice, criticism, and hostility, and threatens to end the relationship. Such acts function as a safety-valve, simulating reciprocity for the recipient and giving him a feeling of self-esteem, autonomy, initiative, and improved morale. This whole sequence of events is called *pseudo-reciprocity* rather than *pure reciprocity* because both parties are out of phase with each other and the recipient, who feels more deprived than the donor, resorts to dramatic action to try to liquidate his obligation.

In making such a rough sketch of these two patterns of bilateral gift behavior, I have used numbers (1, 2, 3, etc.) to indicate steps in the sequences of gift behavior and to suggest duration of time.[20]

20. For a more exact treatment of time durations in studying human behavior, see E. D. CHAPPLE, 'The Interaction Chronograph: Its Evolution and Present Application,' *Personnel*, XXV, No. 4, 1949, pp. 295-301, and E. D. CHAPPLE and C. M.

A simple schematic to suggest a *kula*-type or circular reciprocity system follows the first two types. Such a design may be considered a prototype for organizing technical assistance relationships which provide 'welbalanced chains of reciprocal services.' Empirical studies of the United Nations' technical assistance experience or the less formally organized intra-African efforts (e.g., Mali-Guinea-Ghana) of 1960 would be in order to find out how well contemporary reality fits the *kula* model.

THREE PATTERNS OF GIFT BEHAVIOR
Bilateral Patterns

I. Reciprocity +

II. Pseudo Reciprocity ±

Kula-Type Pattern: Circular Reciprocity

The three patterns of gift behavior just presented are but a few of the possibilities[21] to which researchers and policy-makers might give attention in designing or administering technical assistance programs. If choices of a model were to be made from these three, it appears that the *kula*-type exchange offers better chances than bilateral exchanges for satisfactory reversals of donor and recipient roles, thereby providing a minimum of strain between those who build up obligations by giving and receiving. The case study of B. illustrated pseudo-reciprocity. Its significance for future research and policy lies mainly in exposing the importance of gift-returning of gift-circulating mechanisms, the absence of which can lead to disequilibrium or conflict while gifts of goods, ideas, and techniques are in motion. If bilateral relations persist in technical assistance, the negotiators and planners of aid programs also might consider the implications of the proposition: Consultation, the act of seeking advice and consent on the

ARENSBERG, 'Measuring Human Relations: An Introduction to the Study of Interaction of Individuals,' *Genetic Psychology Monographs*, XXII, 1940, pp. 3-147.
21. For example, a pyramidal pattern might be found in which A gives to B and C, and B in turn gives to D and E, while C gives to F and G. Or tribute given from subordinates to superordinates could be shown on a diagram where A, B, and C, who occupy equivalent positions in a social structure, give upward to D.

part of the donor, can serve as a gift-returning mechanism in human groups where knowledge and intellectual services are valued as exchange commodities. Intangibles thus may replace tangibles as countergifts.

Translated into theory, diagnosis, and prescription, the question about bilateral versus multi-national organization of aid has been given exploratory answers by two proponents of multi-national transmission of goods, services, and knowledge. George Liska, in a theoretical essay on the politics and organization of security, sums up the history of the concept of equilibrium,[22] and concludes that the ultimate goal of scientists and statesmen ('the good life of individual men in free communities, great or small') can best be found through interdependence. He favors a United Nations versus a bilateral policy for technical assistance.[23]

A sharper recommendation for the same policy, and a proposal about which research needs yet to be done, comes from Margaret Mead:

... Point Four operations are not yet our best invention ... In giving technical assistance today ... we have the choice of acting bilaterally, as members of a single, very rich, very prosperous, very generous, but necessarily self-interested ... nation-state, or as members of an associated group of nations, in which we who wish to help and they who need help meet in an equality of interest and dignity.... Within the ... United Nations ... it is one member of a group of brothers asking help from their own group, not the poor asking the rich, or the weak the strong, or the unskilled the technically trained.[24]

22. See GEORGE LISKA, *International Equilibrium* (Cambridge, Mass.: Harvard University Press, 1957). He traces the various uses of the equilibrium concept by George Catlin, Harold Laswell, Talcott Parsons, Joseph Schumpeter, and Chester Barnard.
23. Little is left out of his description of the goals of the United Nations as a design for peace: 'Among the goals (of the UN) is a balanced development of interdependent areas of concern such as food and industrial resources, health and productivity, technical skills and more general education, diffusion and mutual adaptation, rather than unilateral imposition, of skills, techniques, and standards in technical, educational, health, labor, and other matters; and the discovery of a common denominator, rather than a premature synthesis, in the realm of cultural and ideological differences in general, and in matters such as human – including political and social – rights in particular.' (*Ibid.*, p. 127.)
24. See MARGARET MEAD, 'Christian Faith and Technical Assistance,' in WAYNE H. COWAN, ed., *What the Christian Hopes for in Society* (New York: Association Press, 1957), pp. 91-92. With Dr. Mead's hope in mind that UN aid has the chance to help wipe out discrepancies between the giver and receiver, it would be interesting to study UN technical assistance operations to find out how well these fit the *kula*-type pattern of circular reciprocity. A related question is whether there are *kula*-type relationships to be found in the United States' 'third country' programs in which, for example, American money would finance Denmark's training of Indonesians in agricultural cooperatives or France would take over some of the Americans' stated obligation to teach improved productivity methods to the Yugoslavs.

Whatever organizational arrangements are invented for future sharing and distribution of the world's technical and intellectual resources, it seems clear that we will need to develop an international style of reciprocity. In the *kula*-system or in other intra-cultural traditional exchanges (e.g., food for mats in Polynesia) as well as in intra-cultural giving and receiving and repaying in American culture, a good deal is completely specified and the only thing necessary is to keep to the rules. But when it comes to *international* exchange, one runs straight up against all the complex problems of *different* systems. Does the giver have the right and duty to suggest what return should be made and when? Is it his responsibility to find out what the recipient can and would like to return? These questions have been implicit and partly explicit in this study. A remaining question to which scientists and statesmen should give attention is: 'Would it be better to think of adjusting somehow the different expectations of each of the cultures involved or, instead, to think of developing an international system toward which any exchangers could work, adapting their own cultural style to this rather than to the style of other donors or recipients?'[25]

The United Nations already offers a rich opportunity for studying how well we may have moved toward an international style of give and take.[26] The role of international agencies acting as intermediaries has not yet

25. I am indebted to Dr. Rhoda Métraux for raising this question. (Personal correspondence, January 12, 1961.)

26. In addition to the UN experience, the African scene abounds with opportunities to make further case studies of the giving, receiving, and repaying process as new nation states end their periods of bilateral receiving and search for multi-national relationships in the more complex world of international organizations and coalitions of African states. Israel's aid to Ghana, the Soviet Union's aid to Guinea, and the overtures to Africans from Czechoslovakia and Poland also are part of the giving and receiving networks now being established in Africa outside of the historic colonial relationships. In using Africa as a laboratory for further testing of Mauss' ideas on gift exchange, it may be useful to start with the testimony of a former U.S. aid official in Africa, William E. Moran, Jr., who wrote in personal correspondence, October 21, 1959:

> Africans tend to emphasize how distasteful it is to be usually or regularly the recipient of gifts. They relate this to traditional practices of exchanging gifts in their own society. They relate it specifically to the problem of technical assistance and indicate a feeling that a relationship in which one party is always the giver and the other always the receiver is an unsatisfactory one ... This attitude is not unusual. We found it in Europe with the Technical Assistance program ... We do inevitably gain something in giving technical assistance, if only from the increased general understanding of our people engaged in the process. ... We might be able to show the African that we bring to him not just what we have learned in our own country but what we have learned in other countries and take back to our own country and these other countries what we have learned in working with him ... U.S. government people have difficulty because they are 'forbidden' to accept gifts.

been analyzed, to my knowledge, from the standpoint of a theory of obligation. Much remains to be discovered empirically and analytically about the nature of differences in cultural perceptions of 'strings attached' to gifts. We may find ourselves re-discovering the validity of Mauss in yet another context, concluding again perhaps that 'stringless gifts are myths, that there are no free or pure gifts in any donor-recipient relationship.'

We have yet to study the mental health and education implications of such a statement. With B. representing concretely a whole system of variables operating in international technical assistance, we at least have a specific basis from which to speculate and study these implications for both individuals and nations. In the new decade of the 1960's, the case of Monsieur B. provides a special reminder of a question asked by a British anthropologist during World War II: 'What dignified role is each of the various nations best fitted to play? . . . What motivational patterns shall we evoke between those who give and those who receive . . . (in order) to submit not to each other but to some abstract principle?'[27]

Marcel Mauss has put us already on the road to finding some of the answers in describing the processes which primitive and ancient men knew and which industrial men and leaders of the new states are now re-discovering.

27. See G. BATESON, 'Morale and National Character,' in G. WATSON, ed., *Civilian Morale* (Boston: Houghton and Mifflin, 1942), p. 91. One of the patterns of finding dignified roles through complementary or symmetrical relationships has been suggested by another anthropologist, Kalervo Oberg, whose reflections on technical assistance as gift exchange are based on his work as an administrator in Brazil for the International Cooperation Administration. In a memorandum to Washington headquarters, March 8, 1959, he wrote: 'Brazilians respond favorably to aid, whether this is financial, material, or advisory, or all combined, when these elements form part of a joint enterprise to which each contributes according to his capacity or demands of the situation. Doing things together, in partnership, establishes a feeling of equality ... *The good neighbor and true leader is not one who gives presents or advice but one who shares common problems* [italics mine] and works shoulder to shoulder towards their solution as a *primus inter pares*' [italics mine].

EPILOGUE

'Devenons-nous Américains?' asked *L'Express* in a July, 1967 issue showing pictures of Paris drugstores on the Champs-Elysees and the Boulevard St. Germain, along with American-made IBM computers in labs, and the presence of suburban supermarkets. This was the year of debate over the 'technology gap,' symbolized by Jean-Jacques Servan-Schreiber's *Le Défi Américain*, and the removal of NATO headquarters from French soil, with the accompanying pride-producing ability of the French to pay hard cash for the buildings and equipment left behind. It was the year when Prime Minister Lester B. Pearson of Canada found 'unacceptable' President Charles de Gaulle's promise to support 'liberty, equality and fraternity' for French-speaking Canadians – an act which earned de Gaulle the sympathy of Tass, the Soviet news agency, for helping Frenchmen keep their 'national character' despite American power, while at the same time prompting *Le Monde* to complain of de Gaulle's 'pathological superego.' It was the period when Art Buchwald, the humorist, in an imaginary conversation with his friend Zimmerman, learned that de Gaulle would allow Great Britain into the Common Market the moment the Americans sent word to de Gaulle, through a neutral power, that the greatest fear of the United States is that France *will* permit the British to have their membership.[1] It was also an epoch when some French citizens, even if anti-Gaullist, found eternal truths in the dialogues about gratitude and obligations in Montherlant's theatrical piece, *Malatesta*.

In his *Manuel d'ethnographie*, a summary of his Paris lectures from 1926 to 1939, Marcel Mauss encouraged his students to focus on such concrete situations in order to see 'the whole.' He urged them to have a sense for 'acts and the relations between them,' and for 'proportions and connections.' That counsel, if followed even in a random manner today in taking a new look at what is going on in the Atlantic community,' allows the armchair student of French reactions to the New World to find, in the

---

1. Cf. Art Buchwald, 'How to Cope with de Gaulle? Why, Kill Him with Kindness,' *Washington Post*, Jan. 4, 1968.

late 1960's, clear continuities with the near past of the 1950's. President de Gaulle's efforts to rid the French of their obligations and dependence on American protection and benefactions have reached such a crescendo in 1968 that Prime Minister Pompidou has appealed to the U.S. government to assure the American people, some of them engaged in voluntary boycotts against French goods, that the French have no systematic, organized program of hostility against the United States.

The concepts of 'antagonistic acculturation' and 'natavistic revival'[2] have lost none of their usefulness in understanding the French quest for reciprocity, and an escape from being the 'poor guests' at an American potlatch feast at which the well-intentioned host fails to make clear that his generosity is for his own pleasure and good. While it is simplistic to 'explain' Gaullism merely as revenge against American failure to practice French notions of reciprocity, I am sufficiently impressed by what seems to be a congruence between Maussian gift theory[3] and Gaullist practice that I wonder if it would be useful, in future research on the gift behavior of nations, to identify such phenomena as 'the Gaullist effect.'

If the 'Gaullist effect' proves inadequate as a short-hand way of labelling national drives toward autonomy, or resistance to another nation's benevolent hegemony, (could it apply, for example, to Rumania's walk-out from the Soviet-sponsored consultative meeting of Warsaw Pact states in Budapest?[4]), students may wish nevertheless to investigate France's own handling of her foreign aid and cultural relations in order to have further confirmation of how she – and perhaps many other nations – would have preferred to have been treated by affluent outsiders in a moment of need. 'Une coopération, non une "assistance,"' is the theme of the communiqué following a visit to Quebec of Alain Peyrefitte, de Gaulle's minister of education, in September, 1967). 'Les mots d'"entraide", d'"égalité" et de "réciprocité" ont constitué le véritable leitmotiv des conversations ...'[5] The communiqué emphasized that Quebec is not an underdeveloped country, but an adult country which could give to France as much as it received. What France could give Quebec would be an opening on the outside

2. Cf. A. L. KROEBER, 'Nativism, Revivals and Messiahs' in *Anthropology* (New York: Harcourt, Brace and Co., 1948), pp. 437-444.
3. A new appreciation of the significance of Mauss' masterpiece, *The Gift*, is found in Steven Lukes' biographical article, 'Marcel Mauss,' in David L. Sills, ed., *International Encyclopedia of the Social Sciences* (New York: Crowel-Collier MacMillan, 1968).
4. Cf. Anatole Shub, 'Rumania Pulls Out of Red Conference,' *Washington Post*, March 1, 1968, and Henry Kamm, 'Warsaw Pact Nations Open Conference in Sofia,' *New York Times*, March 7, 1968.
5. Cf. 'Les Échanges Culturels Franco-Québécois Seront Considérablement Accrus,' *Le Monde*, 17-18 September, 1967, p. 20.

world after two centuries of an asphyxiated and morose life, a chance to fight against invading grip of the economic and cultural strength of the anglo-saxons. Yet, France would take numerous advantages from the cooperation, one of them being, through the intermediary role of Quebec, contact with the methods and technology of the Americans which flow through the universities – hydrology, medical sciences, forestry, the science of organization. And if it were not clear enough to Quebec's southern neighbors that the French insist on reciprocity in their transactions inside and outside France, we should take note of the toast de Gaulle offered to U.S. Ambassador Charles Bohlen at his departure from Paris January 30, 1968. In that farewell, de Gaulle referred to the 200-year-old friendship between the two countries, taking note of frictions as well as a mutually rewarding balancing act which historically has meant that when each has, at times, led a hazardous life through 'an impulse of power' the other has insisted on moderation.[6] The implication was that now, in Vietnam where de Gaulle views darkly the American role, France is in a position, having been there, too, to remind us of her good example, (i.e., withdrawal) hoping that we might accept her 'gift' to moderate our 'impulse.'

Though France now takes pride in having reversed her colonial role, notably in Indochina and Algeria, French economic relationship with tropical Africa also emphasize cooperation and not assistance. The French foreign aid program, handled by the Ministry of Cooperation, bears close study for its explicit *quid pro quo* arrangements which make clear to both African and French parties what is being given and what is being received or exchanged. Former President Nkrumah of Ghana, used to call these arrangements 'neo-colonialism,' but France has achieved, for the time being, a pragmatic working relationship with her former colonies. 'France continues to supply more aid to independent Africa than Russia and the United States combined – but there is no nonsense about "no strings,"' according to one recent reporter.[7] In contrast, the U.S. emphasizes aid, and

6. The reader will recall in the main text of this study references to how Monsieur 'B' and other Frenchmen reacted to American restraints on both the French and the British at the time of the 1956 Suez crisis. More than a decade later, French 'restraints' on American power took many forms, among them the role of France in the gold crisis of the spring of 1968 with its threat to the value of the American dollar. He said: 'It certainly seems that there is always one of our two countries whose instinct inclines it to moderation when the other tends to abandon moderation. At the various times when France was choosing to lead a hazardous life, she did not unfailingly have the United States' support. Today, when the latter in its turn is particularly susceptible to the impulses of power, it is true that France does not always approve of it. Perhaps ... these divergences ... have contributed to world equilibrium.' Cf. French Embassy press release, No. 281, New York, February 1, 1968.
7. Russell Warren Howe, 'The Third Empire in Africa,' *Baltimore Sun*, February 20, 1968.

seems embarrassed at speaking of 'strings' or even enlightened self-interest.

If there are continuities in the gift culture of the French, so are there persisting styles of American reactions to 'gift situations' both within the national society and beyond. Take first an example from the domestic U.S. scene. The rioting of 'ghetto' dwellers in 164 U.S. communities during the summer of 1967 produced a call for a domestic Marshall Plan to deal with poverty. At the same time one heard the rioters charged with ingratitude because they felt no obligation to be thankful for either civil rights legislation or public investment in urban renewal and slum clearance from earlier years. A National Advisory Commission on Civil Disorders in 1968 called for a 'compassionate, massive and sustained national action to prevent America from becoming "two societies, one black, one white, separate and unequal."' Though the report recognized the demoralizing effect of welfare and recommended creation of 550,000 jobs and 500,000 housing units, little or no attention was given to what impoverished Negroes or poor whites might contribute to the national good in the way of talent, skilled manpower, or ultimate purchasing power. Instead, the main focus of public attention to the report was on a *mea culpa* statement of 'white racism.' The best-intentioned public servants, publicists and legislators still remained oblivious to the hazards of charity and pity. Unless accompanied by an attiude hat the recipient has something to offer, the donor group, i.e., the more affluent majority acting through public officials, presents new opportunities for social conflict when it acts benevolently expecting in return gratitude and docility. A theory of gifts and obligations might help produce, both for the majority and minority, a more palatable form of social contact, free from 'backlash' of various colors.

Other signs exist of a durable trait in American culture which might be called a moral blockage of reciprocity: the fear of obligations implied by gifts. On the domestic scene, newspapers abound daily with stories of gifts which produce court cases of 'conflict of interests,' causing resignation of public officials or disqualifications of those nominated. Moreover, the United States Congress, in October, 1966, passed the Foreign Gifts and Decorations Act which states that Government employees must surrender gifts worth over fifty dollars. The Chief of Protocol of the Department of State presides as curator over gifts from visiting heads of state which are considered, because of the law, too valuable to be kept by the public officials to whom they were offered. These include diamonds and leopard skins given to the Vice-President and Mrs. Hubert Humphrey during their trip to Africa. As in France, but in marked contrast of styles, one finds a certain match in the United States between the handling of gifts and obligations within the society and the attitudes and laws which restrain our receptivity to gifts coming from the outside world.[8]

Despite a culturally influenced awkwardness in handling obligations arising out of gifts given, and our innocence about recipients, desires also to be donors, some U.S. officials, notably Secretary of State Dean Rusk, have clear views about reciprocity in war and in negotiations for peace.[9] American verbal efforts to bring an end to the Vietnam war have been marked by repeated statements emphasizing the need for reciprocal actions, e.g., withholding bombing in exchange for non-infiltration by North Vietnamese and Vietcong. In the quiet of the reconstruction period after the war, an international team of social scientists should be organized to make a clinical study of verbal and military interactions of the various parties to the conflict. Thus we might find out if cultural differences, as distinct from ideological or power positions, can explain, in part, the way the different contestants have behaved in response to the others' conditions and offers of the 'gifts' of peace. Parallel to a study on cross-cultural factors affecting negotiation and bargaining should be another on how revenge, honor, and rewards and punishments are perceived in the different cultures and sub-cultures represented in the war.[10] Finally, the team might also try to document the evolution of a nascent 'Gaullist effect' among South Vietnamese who, burdened by their incredible 'debt' to their outside benefactors, were showing signs of seeking autonomy and expressing hostility toward their American protectors.

8. Gifts nevertheless come into the United States from various nations and are highly honored and accepted: Algeria's gift of money to the Kennedy library at Harvard University; Egypt's gift of a Nile temple to be installed in New York; Japan's gold brocade and Italy's marble for the Kennedy Center for the Performing Arts in Washington; African offers of scholarship for Americans to study in African universities, and France's gift to Atlanta of a Rodin sculpture.

9. While president of the Rockefeller Foundation, and before the agony of the Vietnam war preoccupied his diplomatic career, Rusk was questioned in Washington about his views on the psychological and ideological weakness of the United States in its external relations. He replied: 'It doesn't seem to me that we can improve our psychological position significantly merely by saying something else to people than we have been saying. It seems that our psychological position can be improved by doing a lot of the jobs we are doing a little better and by working toward more of a sense of reciprocity between some of these countries and ourselves ... For example ... I would be tempted to see us appoint a Deputy Director of the International Co-operation Administration in charge of receiving assistance, and try to stimulate a country like India, or Burma, or Indonesia ... to consider what contributions they can make to the enrichment of American life and culture ...' Cf. 'United States Readiness for War,' 27 April, 1959, Publication No. L59-139, Industrial College of the Armed Forces, Washington, D.C., 1958-59.

10. A framework for understanding honor as a social value is to be found in Julian Pitt-Rivers' article on 'honor' in David L. Sills, ed., International Encyclopedia of the Social Sciences (New York: Crowell-Collier MacMillan, 1968).

In reviewing contemporary events illustrating the eternal verities of Mauss' generalizations, I should also take advantage of fresh historical perspective on gift happenings in the late 1960's – whether in foreign affairs or domestic race relations. Prof. Michael Kenny, a student of Hispanic civilization and its spread from Spain to the New World, has told me, in personal correspondence, that Mauss' triad of obligations – giving, receiving and repaying – lies 'right in the heart of almsgiving and the concept of medieval socialism.' The Spanish beggar even today will ask you forthfrightly (in no way a 'beggarly' manner): 'Alms for the love of God,' to which in former times the man approached would answer: 'Forgive me brother,' for one never knew when the tables would be turned. The final comment of the triad, Kenny says, is not in the thanks of the beggar nor in his offer to repay, which he obviously cannot do in the foreseeable future, but simply: 'God will repay you.' This sort of thing, like medieval socialism, takes it out of the realm of charity into the obligatory nature of justice. 'I see no reason,' Kenny wrote, 'why this could not apply at the international level.'

Until future historical, sociological and economic perspectives can come from more empirical research on the obligations to give, receive and repay, I offer these propositions as points of departure:

1. People in old, traditional civilizations generally are careful about paying back gifts. They are uncomfortable if they see no way to discharge an obligation, and this discomfort can take the form of withdrawal from, or resentment and hostility against, the original donor.

2. People who have been regarded as teachers do not like to return permanently to the status of pupils. Teaching is a form of giving and learning is analogous to receiving. If people are long deprived of a chance to teach and give, they will create situations, at the risk of offending, in order to end their deprivations.

3. The gifts any nation expects in return for aid (especially rich and powerful nations like the U.S. and the U.S.S.R.) do not always match the gifts which the receiving nation feels are best to offer, e.g., gratitude, permission to station troops, votes in the United Nations, or 'anti-communist' or 'anti-capitalist' postures.

4. Gratitude is the least of the gifts donor nations should expect. Recipients are never grateful until they can render something they value. Expectation of gratitude alienates the donor from the recipient.

5. Gifts can take the form of material or intellectual and artistic goods. Whereas primitive or pre-literate men reciprocated with a bowl of food, a canoe, or a ceremonial, industrial men can act upon the same universal desires (to get rid of obligations) by offering machines, scientific knowledge, ideas, techniques and suggestions. Consultation can serve as a

gift-returning mechanism. Status and power differences between the donor and receiver produce less strain when the donor asks the receiver to participate in decisions which affect them both.

6. Future leadership in any alliance must rest on an imaginative seeking of a variety of gifts from the people who want to give them, but who do not know how. The more leaders solicit advice and show willingness to listen unpeevishly to criticism and suggestions, the greater their own knowledge of their self-interest and the greater the self-esteem of their allies.

7. Whether 'primitive' or 'industrial,' societies can show signs of 'nativistic revival.'[11] With primitive tribes, this appears when the shock of cultural contact with outsiders (donors) is often sudden and severe, when hunting lands or pastures are taken away or broken under the plow, where holy places are profaned. At this point, a prophet is likely to arise, and the ancestral dead are to return. Gaullism may provide, through an understanding of the 'Gaullist effect,' a striking parallel.[12]

July, 1968   McLean, Virginia, U.S.A.

11. Though not dealing with nativism, a valuable contribution to understanding its social underpinnings in pre-literate communities is MARSHALL D. SAHLINS, 'On the Sociology of Primitive Exchange,' in A.S.A. Monographs 1, (London: Tavistock Publications; New York: Frederick A. Praeger, 1965) pp. 139-236. I regret it was not available to me during the writing of this book.
12. The notion of the 'Gaullist effect' even may be applied, paradoxically, to understanding some aspects of the anti-Gaullist manifestations within France during the strikes of students and workers in May and June, 1968. Apart from French official blame for the troubles on Communists, could one other interpretation be the view that the strikes represented the very kind of 'ungrateful' impatience against de Gaulle's benevolent, paternal protection of the French people that de Gaulle, on behalf of those same people, demonstrated against the 'Anglo-Saxons'? Could reciprocity between the leader and certain dissident segments of the population be restored by the leader's promise that 'participation' would become the guiding principle of 'a renewed France'? Could the leader's 'gift' of willingly staying in office bring a countergift of social peace? Hostility and revenge against the leader's benefactions to the nation (his selfless offers, and achievements, in 'saving' France repeatedly) also might be interpreted as a variant on the theme of the prodigal son: errant 'children' (students and workers) challenge paternal authority, are met with hurt silence and then threats of punishment, and finally 'forgiven' after paternal authority is tenuously restored. It remains to be seen whether the national family can find a new equilibrium through yet another charismatic 'prophet' who might demonstrate the 'Gaullist effect' by rising up to repudiate de Gaulle's 'hegemony' over French society. Such a new leader thus would 'restore' France to her glorious old traditions of noisy parliamentary government, or that other traditional republican value of wiping the social slate clean through revolution—the kind of revolution de Gaulle has led within an Atlantic community dominated by the United States. The interplay between de Gaulle's domestic and foreign roles is described in HENRY TANNER: 'De Gaulle Role in World Affairs viewed as Shaken,' New York Times, June 28, 1968.

AFTERWORD TO THE TRANSACTION EDITION: THE ULTIMATE GIFT*

In Western civilization, perhaps the worst-case scenario of one group's presenting a monumental gift to another involved the legendary Trojan horse.[1] A Trojan prince, Paris, fell in love with Helen, the beautiful wife of the king of Sparta. Helen fled, or was forced to flee, to Troy. The Greeks swore vengeance on Paris and on Troy. For ten years, they laid siege to Troy but could not take the city. They built a huge wooden horse. Greek soldiers hid in the horse while the rest of the Greeks pretended to sail away. The curious Trojans dragged the horse inside the city walls, despite a priest's warning "I fear the Greeks, even when bringing gifts." That night, the Greek soldiers crept out of the horse, opened the city gates, and let in their compatriots to loot and burn the Asia Minor city. The legends outlive the archaeological evidence.

In striking contrast, during the presidency of Grover Cleveland (1885-89), the French left outside the "gates" of New York a gift of even more monumental proportions. Instead of soldiers inside, the French brought a skeleton for Miss Liberty that represented the state of the art of French civil engineering: Gustave Eiffel's iron frame, influenced by his earlier designs for bridges. The outside skin revealed breathtaking beauty, as art and engineering became one. The curious New Yorkers did not drag the statue into Manhattan, though she had stood earlier in the streets of Paris, as shown in the famous Victor Dargaud painting of 1883.

The long buildup in France in preparing for the offering of the gift had made Miss Liberty a part of the French national consciousness. Though motivated by enlightened self-interest – to find allies in the preservation

---

* This chapter was originally published in Wilton S. Dillon and Neil G. Kotler, eds., *The Statue of Liberty Revisited: Making a Universal Symbol* (Washington and London: Smithsonian Institution Press, 1994). Reprinted by permission of Smithsonian Institution Press.

of republican government in France – the French donors found their countrymen attaching great value to the gift as the symbolic rays of light found their way into French popular culture, much as the statue would do for generations after her arrival in the United States. James Tissot's painting *Ces Dames des chars* reveals the delight that French circus fans took in Liberty's image.

The French ship of war *Isere* transported the statue to New York. Miss Liberty traveled the ocean in two hundred separate crates. The unveiling of the completed Statue of Liberty prompted a spectacular demonstration and parade on Liberty Day, October 28, 1886, with soldiers, sailors, and civilians marching on lower Broadway while Navy ships formed a flotilla in the harbor. Millions of visitors have since become pilgrims to the island to admire and climb inside one of the wonders of the world.

The Statue of Liberty remains the ultimate gift of one nation to another. Of all the gifts that have come to us, we may never have anything to compare with a gift of such scale, tangibility, and symbolism as the Statue of Liberty. What other nation has given a major national symbol to another and thus contributed to the identity and self-esteem of both?

French anthropology has focused on females as commodities of exchange or as targets of seizure in tribal warfare, leading to a lot of pushing and shoving to get the females home again. Coming from a civilization that prizes women, ranging from adoration of the Virgin Mary to Jeanne d'Arc and the ladies in Renoir's paintings, the Statue of Liberty gains new meaning in light of the feminist movement. Can our symbol inspire the liberation of women from household drudgery and the achievement of equal opportunity in the workplace? Liberty was not captured by a warring tribe and taken forever from her kith and kin, like the white woman in *Dances with Wolves*. She was offered to us in peace, purely as a gift. She has become a part of our psyche and ethos, a vital party to the delicate balancing act between feminine, masculine, and androgynous elements in our own cultures, and we are not about to let her go. She serves as a daily reminder that we live on a very small planet and that our motives to get along with each other are stronger when bonded by a beautiful piece of sculpture than by military force.

One of the universal maxims of gift giving and receiving is that both parties should attach value to the gift. We Americans have so internalized and appropriated the gift of Liberty as our own self-image, according her a stature shared only by Uncle Sam and the bald eagle, that we have almost forgotten where the gift of Miss Liberty came from. Victor Turner, in his *Forest of Symbols*, observes that "the significant elements of a symbol's meaning are related to what it does and what is done to it by and for whom."[2]

Liberty Enlightening the World, as the Statue of Liberty was named by its creator, Frédéric-Auguste Bartholdi, stands in voluptuous contrast to the bald eagle, an earlier and concurrent American symbol. Indeed, there is a majesty in both symbols, and both have roots deep in classical antiquity. Roman warriors used a golden figure of an eagle as a sign of strength and bravery. Russian and Austrian emperors also had their eagles. Although the United States was anti-imperial at birth, the bald eagle was chosen as the national bird in 1782. For all the years between 1795 and 1933 we minted a $10 gold coin that showed an eagle clutching a laurel wreath. The eagle, however, has been eclipsed symbolically by the Statue of Liberty. While the bird itself continues to receive well-deserved attention from preservationists to prevent extinction, much psychocultural analysis remains to be done on the comparative strength of Uncle Sam, the bewhiskered male figure best known for recruiting in the military.

New Yorker cartoonist Peter Steiner told me that he found Liberty and Uncle Sam so different, appealing to different parts of a citizen's psyche, that he could not imagine putting them in the same frame. However, another *New Yorker* artist, Mischa Richter, has recently domesticated the two. One cartoon, of February 23, 1992, shows Liberty reclining in one lounge chair and Uncle Sam snoozing in another, with a tea table between them. In the caption Liberty is saying, "We have no friends, just allies." A sequel, on March 23, 1992, shows an upright Uncle Sam opening a refrigerator in the kitchen. On its doors are mottoes like "The only thing we have to fear is fear itself," "Give me liberty or give me death," and "A house divided against itself cannot stand." Liberty, reading a newspaper in the background, holds high her cup of coffee. A third cartoon, on April 27, 1992, in what now seems a genre, shows Liberty lounging with a newspaper, crown spikes aloft, feet on a footstool, listening to Uncle Sam, who is sitting in a neighboring chair and holding a cup of coffee, confess, "I have something to get off my chest – I don't know the words to the second verse of 'The Star-Spangled Banner'!"

The two images already had been joined in cartoons in the late nineteenth century, first showing Uncle Sam delivering money to Liberty for her pedestal and later depicting Uncle Sam standing at the foot of Liberty to welcome immigrants to Ellis Island. A further examination of our own culture will clarify how this extraordinary symbol with roots in the ancient past became part of our pantheon of "American" symbols (which also includes Coca-Cola and blue jeans).

THE 1986 RITE OF PASSAGE

Awash in all kinds of symbols, the beautifully restored gift statue at the celebrations on Independence Day, July 4, 1986, was surrounded below by officials and citizens and ships floating at her feet and above by dirigibles and jets flying over in formation. Her hundredth birthday brought President François Mitterrand, chief of the donor state, which evolved out of ancient kingdoms and remnants of the Roman Empire, to meet with President Ronald Reagan. As the head of another of the world's great republics, Reagan symbolized the continuing experiment with democracy and the shared philosophical antecedents from Greece and, later, the Enlightenment period in France.

The philosophical dimensions of the occasion were eclipsed by a stately procession of tall ships, a replay of the July 4, 1976, pageantry marking the bicentennial of the Declaration of Independence. The French president's visit was scarcely noticed by the *New York Times*. Perhaps Liberty had become so "Americanized," so domesticated,[3] that it was hard to remember who gave her and how she got here. President and Madame Mitterrand did appear, however, at a spectacular pageant on Governor's Island, and they dined with the Reagans and members of the Cabinet.

A FRENCH ANTHROPOLOGIST LOOKS AT GIFTS

The gift of the statue needs to be understood in the context of more than two hundred years of reciprocity between France and the United States. Marcel Mauss (1872-1950), a famous French anthropologist and linguist, provides a framework for understanding such exchanges in his classic 1924 "Essai sur le don," translated into English as *The Gift*.[4] It draws on his studies of ancient civilizations, including Israel, Greece, Rome, Scandinavia, India, and China, as well as contemporary preliterate societies. From the study of all these groups, Mauss generalized three universal types of human obligations: the obligation to give, the obligation to receive, and the obligation to repay. These are fundamental and highly developed characteristics of most cultures, but they have particular significance in French civilization.

In my fieldwork in France, I found strong evidence of reciprocal ties between parents and children, friends and lovers, and families. These patterns extended to the workplace and, beyond that, to the nation.[5] A clear sense of history, in addition, helps French citizens remember what their nation has given, received, and repaid, whether the nation is governed through monarchial or republican forms. We Americans seem to lack a similar social inventory of gift bookkeeping. Our relatively short history, even ahistoricity, may explain why some of our rhythms of exchange are irregular or asymmetrical.

Extrapolating from Mauss's theories of reciprocity, I hope that future historians of United States-French relationships will rethink and reinterpret our interdependent histories through the lens of a gift-exchange metaphor. In the meantime, with Miss Liberty much in mind, I suggest we need to start with a look at the triangular relationships among Britain, France, and America. Reality would be ignored if relationships among the three were studied bilaterally.

For whatever the motives (the centuries-old rivalry between France and Britain, as manifest in Shakespeare's *Henry V?*), I think the first great gift the French ever presented to the United States was a recognition of the country's right to exist – still a live issue in the world, one that haunts today's Arab-Israeli rivalry in the Middle East and fuels the tensions over the creation of a Palestinian state.

THE GIFT OF YORKTOWN

The first act – from our first ally – of recognition of our national independence from Great Britain came from France. The fact that France at the time was at war with Britain and that the American rebels were being freed from British masters meant that this validation was a by-product of the Anglo-French war. It nevertheless provided us with a practical basis on which our sovereign existence and separate identity depended. I refer, of course, to the great military triumph at the Battle of Yorktown in 1781. To join with General Washington, Rochambeau's armies came down all the way from Newport, Rhode Island, to the York River, in Virginia, and combined with Admiral François-Joseph-Paul de Grasse's fleet of French ships, which bottled the British ships. The French military action resulted in Cornwallis's surrender.[6]

That extraordinary, primordial gift of both money and manpower, military power and genius, helped pave the way for American independence. It set the stage for long-term reciprocities that endure today, despite occasional troubles growing out of cultural differences in the way we and the French view gifts and respond to those gifts.

An 1889 history text on France written by an American, David H. Montgomery, is a rare recognition of the American debt to France: "In her zeal for the cause of America, France seemed for a time to forget her own misery, and bankrupt though she was, she raised nine millions of francs as a gift to assist the armies of the new-born republic, besides furnishing about fifteen millions more as a loan. In addition...the Marquis de Lafayette, a young man of 20, loaded a vessel with arms and munitions of war at his own expense, and sailed for America to offer his services to General Washington."[7]

French contributions were not only financial and logistical. The thought of French philosopher Jean-Jacques Rousseau was embodied in the affirmation of the Declaration of Independence that "all men are created equal." The French officers and soldiers who fought under the American flag returned home inspired with a revolutionary zeal, thus restoring Rousseau's influence to France, after it had been tested and made operational in the New World. Still, Louis XVI, having inherited the burden of the exhausting wars fought by Louis XIV and Louis XV, incurred a debt of $1.3 billion in his war with England on behalf of America. Republican ideas and money crises drove the French Revolution that followed. (The French have never forgotten that their monarchy was weakened by the money that Louis XVI and his officers spent on those New World battles, thereby triggering the Revolution.) Similarly, republican ideas were to motivate Edouard-René Lefebvre de Laboulaye decades later in proposing the Statue of Liberty as a gift from France to celebrate the centennial of the July 4 Declaration of Independence.

The late great French historian, Fernand Braudel (1902-85), shared with me, in various conversations in France and in the United States, his views of history as a series of long-term increments, little bits and pieces of human experience not necessarily related to changes in dynastic rule or wars or revolutions.[8] Thus a Maussian view of more than two hundred years of French-American relationships would require consideration of both a big picture of symbolic gift exchange and snapshots of smaller, lesser-known exchanges. For example, in 1778 France became the first nation to salute an American man-of-war ship, the *Ranger*, commanded by John Paul Jones. Americans later gave to France the ship *America*. After Lafayette fought on the colonialists' side and helped Franklin and Jefferson, a grateful United States gave him a land grant in Louisiana in 1803, and Congress voted to give him $200,000 and a Florida township during his 1824 return visit. Such small reciprocities are interspersed with the big ones: the Louisiana Purchase (made for such a "good price" that fifteen states were formed from the region, thus doubling the size of the country); the Statue of Liberty; military aid in two world wars; and the Marshall Plan. History has yet to pass judgment on the mutuality of EuroDisneyland.

Transactions between heads of state and exchanges in a highly personalized form make up a tapestry of gifts and obligations, both conscious and implicit, that continues to interact with other influences on the way we think, dress, eat, romance, assess each other's "national character," and form alliances. We find a good example of the fusion of personal and national identities in General Charles de Gaulle's restoring France's sense of grandeur in the twentieth century. His was a heroic effort to repair reciprocity after the long periods of damaged self-esteem brought on by war, military occupation, and debts. Gaullist citizens identifying with their leader felt better for his actions, thus completing a circuit linking individuals with the nation.[9] De Gaulle reached far back in time to restore that sense of grandeur, France's *mission civilisatrice*, and made Frenchmen proud to be reminded of another historian's (François Guizot's) observation that "there is hardly any great idea, hardly any great principle of civilization, which has not had to pass through France in order to be disseminated."[10] Yorktown and the Statue of Liberty then were part of recent French memory, links in a chain of history going back to the Roman conquest of Gaul.

I mentioned earlier that French historical consciousness contrasts with our own inventory of who owes to whom and what needs to be repaid. History is important to us, too, but our time perspective is distorted by a deliberate desire to start afresh, a tabula rasa attitude befitting what early settlers perceived as an empty continent. If history is to a nation what memory is to an individual, we Americans suffer occasional amnesia about what we owe to others. We prefer the roles of donor and teacher to those of recipient and pupil.

For example, the bicentennial of the Battle of Yorktown was vividly anticipated in France and almost totally ignored in the United States until the Smithsonian Institution was urged by the American ambassador to France, Arthur Hartman, to compensate for the indifference he was finding in the White House, the Department of State, and Congress. Hartman advised us to prepare our republic for a celebration that would live up to French expectations. "Each time I see President Giscard d'Estaing," the ambassador told me, "he asks what we are doing to prepare for October 18, 1981, and I am embarrassed to have no answers." Through a last-minute convening of interested parties, who met on neutral turf at the Smithsonian, and with the considerable influence of a historically minded Secretary of the Army, the Honorable John O. Marsh, Jr., and the Daughters of the American Revolution, Smithsonian Secretary S. Dillon Ripley and I managed to set a number of commemorations in motion.

Newly elected President Reagan finally invited newly elected President Mitterrand to speak in Yorktown, along with Lord Hailsham of Britain, who was sought especially to add some humor to the occasion. WIlliam H. G. FitzGerald and Francis Hodsoll of the White House helped raise private funds for a documentary film, for the hospitality in Yorktown shown to the French soldiers and sailors participating in the reenactment, and for the Smithsonian exhibition "By Land and by Sea: Independence with the Help of France." Such ad hoc approaches to remembering and fulfilling our historic obligations contrast sharply with the timetables of history guarded by, say, the French Ministry of Culture and a well-educated citizenry with a collective memory. French citizens living in Washington helped keep alive our awareness of French contributions through such organizations as the Lafayette-Rochambeau Society. They provided leadership in erecting at the battlefield site a temporary equestrian statue of General Washington, Rochambeau, and Lafayette by the sculptor Felix W. de Welden.

Marcel Mauss articulates his proposition that one is obliged to receive what is given as follows: "To refuse to give...is like refusing to accept – the equivalent of a declaration of war; it is a refusal of friendship and intercourse."[11] For various internal reasons, the Americans (mainly New Yorkers) organized to receive the Statue of Liberty, like those offering it, had good reason to value it. The New York Union League and later the Century Association became the locus of American efforts to create the American Committee, to secure the site and to oversee the construction, installation, and dedication. Bartholdi, the statue's creator, knew some members of the league and was aware of its commitment to both nationalism and art. Mobilizing the American public to embrace the statue as a symbol of national heritage became the goal of such visionary and pragmatic citizens as John Jay, Richard Butler, William Evarts, James W. Pinchot, Joseph Iasigi, Theodore Weston, Samuel Babcock, Nathan Appleton, Jr., Joseph Drexel, and many others up and down the coast from Boston to Philadelphia. Beauty and symbol became allied with function (it was to serve as a beacon or signal station) and commerce, argued some of the members, who also were eager to celebrate the early and lasting friendship of the two great republics of the nineteenth century. Moreover, the Statue of Liberty would glorify obliquely the preservation of the Union, being created so soon after the Civil War. Bartholdi, aware of the pacific significance of the statue, and not wishing to have his work rub salt in the wounds of the Confederacy, eliminated the

Phyrigian bonnet and downplayed the broken chains that had appeared in earlier versions.

Miss Liberty's American patrons, however, ran into huge difficulties in raising the money needed to build the pedestal on which the statue would rest – the American part of the arrangement to give and to receive. Richard H. Hunt, designer of some New Yorkers' urban palaces and Newport "cottages," the first American to graduate from l'école des Beaux-Arts, had been commissioned to design the pedestal. The task prompted much contentious give-and-take between Hunt and Bartholdi, so that their collaboration also can be understood as uneasy gift exchange in a microcosm.[12]

The pedestal became a symbol in itself for the American obligation to give something to match the French gift. Delays in finding money for it prompted vivid cartoon imagery. An anonymous artist shows Liberty lying on her back, with a floppy-eared Bugs Bunny creature labeled "France" standing guard while awaiting a slow-moving tortoise labeled "Collection Committee" and weighed down by granite slabs identified as "Bartholdi Pedestal?" *Frank Leslie's Illustrated Newspaper* in 1884 shows a toothless, haggard, and decrepit Statue of Liberty, torch and document-bearing arms dropped wearily to her side. Her rays of light are bent and drooping. Birds are shown nesting in the collection box near the first block of the cornerstone. Title: "Statue of Liberty, One Thousand Years Later, Waiting." President Cleveland vetoed federal funds for the pedestal as unconstitutional, but happily presided over the opening ceremony two years later. Americans were not yet accustomed to public subscription as a means of funding sculpture. The Bunker Hill Monument in Boston was not erected until eighteen years after the cornerstone was laid, and Congress had to appropriate money to complete the Washington Monument after the Civil War. Squabbling was rampant over whether the nation, the state, or the city was responsible.

Joseph Pulitzer, fresh from Budapest in 1863, came to the pedestal's rescue. Building on strong earlier support from the American Committee of the Sons of the American Revolution, Pulitzer launched a fundraising crusade through his newspaper, the *New York World*, and successfully raised more than $100,000 in five months' time. He listed names of all contributors. Bartholdi's personal letters to other newspapers were intended to help demonstrate the power of the press in generating public support for the pedestal. Parisian journals saw the delay in raising funds for the pedestal as a lack of American enthusiasm for the statue; one suggested that Liberty stay home and be erected at Le Havre.

Pulitzer's passionate editorial in 1885 reminded Americans of the broad base of French generosity and challenged them to match it. "The $250,000 that the making of the Statue cost was paid in by the masses of the French people – the working men, the tradesmen, the shopgirls, the artisans – by all, irrespective of class or condition. Let us respond in like manner. Let us not wait for the millionaires to give this money." So the committee collected $121,000 from 121,000 people, as Pulitzer bombarded the millionaires with insults – "a poor man's chance to one-up the rich."[13] American honor was saved. However, except for scholars, few Americans I know today seem aware of Pulitzer's role, concentrating instead on his Pulitzer prizes. If America's "common people" who contributed to the statue's pedestal did transmit the stories of it to their descendants, I find few traces of even folkloric memory among fellow citizens today. One encyclopedia, *World Book*, contains no reference at all to Pulitzer's contribution to the Liberty project. Similar discontinuities in recorded memory may prevail in France, but I doubt it. Polling could help verify or deny my hunch. Small but vital details are overshadowed by colossal statues once they are in place and take on a life of their own, independent of their creators or patrons. The National Park Service exhibition at the base of the Statue of Liberty begins to give Pulitzer his due.

Could it be that our national "amnesia" (i.e., about what our nation owes to others) also is related to a culturally determined aversion to being obligated or dependent? Through earlier religious influences, we have developed the notion that it is more blessed to give than to receive, and from our legal system we have derived a tendency to be suspicious of gifts. This suspicion of gift giving is illustrated in Kenneth L. Burns's 1985 documentary on the statue, quoting from the *New York Times* during the campaign in the 1880s to finance the statue's pedestal. The newspaper offered this anonymous quote: "It is ridiculous for Frenchmen to continue to impose on Americans a present they refuse to accept, to worry them with a souvenir that offends them, to humiliate them with a generous idea they do not comprehend, and to beg for thanks that they will not give."

Political campaigns in the United States typically reinforce the commonplace accusations leveled at candidates who accept gifts, incur obligations, and show special favors to their patrons. No other society is so permeated with the concept of "conflict of interest." Yet we are quick to charge others with ingratitude when, after we make a gift overseas, the recipient is found not to be amenable to our wishes.[14] French reactions to the United States Marshall Plan after World War II included popular support for General Charles de Gaulle for his fierce autonomy, which I have compared to "nativistic revivals" in simpler societies. De Gaulle is an example of a leader who emerges to restore a balance of reciprocity and self-esteem vis-à-vis benefactors who do not attach value to what the recipients want to give back.

The Statue of Liberty remains the archetype of a gift offered, a gift received, and a gift "repaid" through two world wars and the Marshall Plan. Healthy alliances are built on the capacity of one donor to reverse the role and become a recipient, and then to give again. As the United States has become a debtor nation through borrowing, and no longer can support an autonomous economy, Americans are having to learn such role reversals.

Happily, some educational endeavors are beginning to teach important history lessons. Two museums have been established to focus on the historic process of Franco-American giving, receiving, repaying. The first is the Musée Blérancourt, founded in 1924 at a seventeenth-century château eighty miles north of Paris. Anne Morgan, daughter of financier J. P. Morgan, whose bank loans to France were repaid, first bought the property in 1917 and made it her headquarters for helping the wounded and homeless in France after World War I. Later, she used the château as a private museum to memorialize mutual aid between France and the United States, and in 1930 she gave the château and her collections to the French government. It is known today as the French National Museum of Franco-American Friendship.

Starting with naval and military battles in which France fought, principally Yorktown, the Blérancourt exhibition treats the great French and American heroes – Washington, Lafayette, Rochambeau, Grasse, John Paul Jones, and others – before focusing on the Treaty of Paris of 1783, which ended the American Revolution. Other themes deal with the British and the French presence in the New World before the Revolution; how American ideas influenced the French Revolution; the Treaty of 1802; the Louisiana sale; the French presence in the United States around 1800 as well as during the rule of Napoleon III, manifested by Lafayette's famous tour, and how we absorbed Bonapartist refugees. The Statue of Liberty is given attention in a pavilion devoted to "America: Land of Liberty." Winding up the nineteenth century, the Musée Blérancourt exhibition takes note of the Industrial Revolution and its effects on both countries, international exhibitions, and the French fascination for American skyscrapers. Yet another pavilion exhibits artworks by American artists in France and French artists in America.

124

The historic Laboulaye family continues to have a hand in the museum, starting with Ambassador André de Laboulaye, a contemporary of Anne Morgan's, and his son, Ambassador François de Laboulaye, the Washington-born diplomat who followed in his father's footsteps, representing France in Washington during the bicentennial at Yorktown and preparing the way for the centennial celebration of the Statue of Liberty.

A second museum that focuses on Franco-American gift exchange is the Statue of Liberty National Monument at Liberty Island, administered by the National Park Service. "The Gift of Friendship" is the banner at the top of a brochure given to today's visitors to the exhibition area of the Statue of Liberty National Museum. Designed by the firm of Chermayoff and Geisman, the exhibition explains how the colossal figure of a woman striding with uplifted flame across the entrance to the New World has become a symbol of America to most people, including Americans. Visitors also can learn that Liberty Enlightening the World was conceived as an expression of French republican ideals, initiated in 1865 by Edouard de Laboulaye, a legal scholar and authority on America. Laboulaye chafed under the repressive regime of Napoleon III and looked admiringly at the United States, a thriving republic that had just survived a civil war and was on the threshold of becoming a prosperous industrial nation. He admired, says the brochure, a nation that had "achieved a delicate balance between liberty and stability that for so long had eluded France." He knew that the statue would be considered subversive inside France, and left it to the gifted Bartholdi to help make Liberty a reality.

Though not a museum, EuroDisneyland features more than Mickey Mouse. The Liberty and Discovery arcade celebrates the creation of the Statue of Liberty, from Bertholdi to the rebirth of Lady Liberty in 1986. This American tribute to the gift may offset some French objections to the Paris-area theme park as a "cultural Chernobyl."

In the more than a century since Liberty became our national icon, the country has passed through earlier objections from the clergy that France had offered us a pagan goddess or else a fatted calf, or that Liberty, with all her Masonic symbols, represented a secret Masonic plot. Various other citizens have dared to look "the gift horse in the mouth." As late as 1925, a Paris newspaper reported that an American pastor, the Reverend Doctor Andrew Bard, had suggested that the Statue of Liberty be replaced by a statue of Christ. The newspaper then added this editorial comment:

Alas, 1,925 years have passed since the son of God vainly tried to illuminate the conscience of man without success. No. The idea of...Dr. Bard is not tenable. We would understand a statue later of Senator LaFollette, or that of a dry America holding a Bible and surrounding by customs officials. We could accept the project of a colossal cowboy, dancing girl, Dempsey or Rockefeller – in short, anything "exciting" – but a statue of Christ, so poor among the poor, erected at the entrance of the country of the dollar and temple of money? No...[s]uch a statue would be capable, all by itself, of slipping away in a day when the White House, influenced by Wall Street bankers, would demand from creditors a little interest for having taken part in the great war for humanity.[15]

Such use of stereotypes and candor by the French can be analyzed as signs of both an enduring and possessive pride in having made such a gift[16] and an intimacy between two quite different peoples who have become "family."

If we move beyond diplomacy, strategy, economics, and intellectual influences over two centuries of history and think of the intangible yet fundamental plane of sentiment and attraction, we will feel as French historian Jean-Baptiste Duroselle did when he wrote, "I do not hesitate to say it: Franco-American relations have never lost the mysterious charm that assures them a place apart in the history of mankind."[17]

Like a great Rorschach test, Liberty has attracted all kinds of interpretations and meanings at different periods of national and world history. A whole book could be written on the perceptions revealed by ceremonial oratory marking the arrival and dedication of the gift in 1886, followed by the fiftieth, seventy-fifth, and hundredth anniversaries. Comparisons and contrasts could be found in the French oratory crafted for those same occasions. One indicator of the overwhelming success of the French gift is the degree to which the statue speaks to differing self-images and national needs of the American people.

At the fiftieth anniversary celebration in 1936, Franklin D. Roosevelt recalled what Grover Cleveland had said half a century earlier on the same spot: "We will not forget that liberty has made here her home...nor shall her chosen altar be neglected."[18] FDR then used what turned out to be prophetic language, as the United States was already having to face the challenge of Hitler and the need for national unity to fight that future war: "The realization that we are all bound together by hope of a common future rather than reverence for a common past has helped us to build on this continent a unity unapproached...in the whole world.... For all our millions of square miles...and people, there is a unity in language and speech, in law and economics, in education and in general purpose, which nowhere finds its match."[19]

126

In the last decade of this century, amid unprecedented ethnic fragmentation, the United States can discover some gifts in the oratory of earlier leaders as we try to rediscover what myths and symbols we hold in common while preserving and celebrating our diversity and our multiple identities. The worldwide commemoration of the 250th anniversary of the birth of Thomas Jefferson in 1993 will provide such an opportunity.

The Statue of Liberty continues her ad valorem mission, bestowing on the world "added value," enriching the donor and the recipient nation together and, indeed, the entire world. On July 4, 1889, the American community in Paris offered the French people a gift of a bronze replica of the Statue of Liberty; it still stands now, on an island in the Seine River, downstream from the Eiffel Tower. In a symbolic sense, this recently restored American gift closes the circle of gift giving that was launched by the French in the 1860s with the gift of Miss Liberty. In a deeper sense, though, the American replica in Paris serves to extend and strengthen the chain of reciprocity between the two peoples that has existed since before the founding of the American Republic and that promises to continue well into the future.

This magnificent exchange of gifts illustrates a declaration delivered by French ambassador Jules J. Jusserand on the occasion of the 1916 ceremony at which Liberty's torch was first lighted with electricity: "Not to a man, not to a nation, the statue was raised. It was raised to an idea – an idea greater than France or the United States: the idea of Liberty."[20]

Contrast that with the Trojan horse!

NOTES

1. A massive mockup of the Trojan horse, made of wood, stands at the entrance of the legendary archaeological site in Hisarlik, Turkey, where tourists may now examine layers of centuries of Greco-Roman cultures. John Fleischman's magazine article "'I Sing of Gods and Men' – and the Stones of Fabled Troy" (*Smithsonian* 22, no. 10 [January 1992]) foreshadowed his current book project about Troy and the human imagination.

2. Victor Turner, the mentor of Barbara Babcock and John MacAloon, whose essay appears in this volume, drew heavily on history and literature in his anthropological career. His *Forest of Symbols*, based on his studies of an African tribe, was published by Cornell University Press in 1967.

3. An example of the domestication of the Statue of Liberty can be found in the Washington private residence of President Woodrow Wilson, now administered by the National Trust for Historic Preservation. A rug depicting American scenes features the Statue of Liberty, the Liberty Bell, the *Mayflower*, Independence Hall, and the Wash-

ington Monument, among other notable "native" sites. The rug lies in Wilson's study and served as a reminder to him, during his long convalescence, of his having presided over the electrification of the statue's beacon in 1916.

4. Originally published as "Essai sur le don, forme et raison de l'échange dans les sociétés archaiques," in *L'Année Sociologique* (1923-24), and given a much wider audience in Claude Lévi-Strauss, ed., *Sociologie et Anthropologie* (Paris: Presses Universitaires de France, 1850); Mauss's ideas eventually reached the English-speaking world in 1954 with a translation by Ian Cunnison, *The Gift* (Glencoe, Ill.: Free Press, 1954).

5. Wilton S. Dillon, *Gifts and Nations: The Obligation to Give, Receive, and Repay*, with a foreword by Talcott Parsons (The Hague and Paris: Mouton, 1968). I discovered Mauss through Lévi-Strauss in Paris in 1951. Decades later, I found Mauss highly relevant to understanding the Statue of Liberty as a key to the gift exchange metaphor in international relations.

6. Howard C. Rice, Jr., and Anne S. K. Brown, trans. and eds., *The American Campaigns of Rochambeau's Army 1780, 1781, 1782, 1783* (Princeton, N.J.: Princeton University Press and Providence, R.I.: Brown University Press, 1972).

7. David H. Montgomery, *The Leading Facts of French History* (Boston: Ginn, 1889).

8. "The short-term is the most capricious and deceptive form of time," Braudel wrote in "History and the Social Sciences," in *Economy and Society in Early Modern Europe: Essays from Annales*, edited by Peter Burke (New York: Harper, 1958). Braudel would have had much to say about contrasting time perspectives of the French and the Americans; the Statue of Liberty indeed gives tangible expression to French preferences for the long term-a gift that lasts.

9. Individuals of different social classes whom I knew in France were attracted to Gaullism as a reminder that France could control her own destiny once again. In my essay "Bonne Année, Oncle Charles" (*New Republic,* January 4, 1964), I explained De Gaulle's independence as not "anti-American" but pro-French, still regarding us as *en famille*, while he was cool and formal with the Soviets with whom he did not "fuss" as much.

10. François Guizat's eight-volume *History of France* (1789-1848) and six-volume *History of the Revolution in England* (1826-56) stimulated nineteenth-century historians to think comparatively of France and the "Anglo-Saxons." David H. Montgomery was a good example.

11. Mauss, *The Gift*, 11.

12. For a richly textured account of that relationship from the perspective of architectural history, see Marvin Trachtenberg, "The Pedestal," in his *Statue of Liberty* (New York: Penguin, 1986). How Bartholdi and Hunt evolved their conceptions for the pedestal is beautifully illustrated in Susan R. Stein, "Richard Morris Hunt and the Pedestal," in *Liberty: The French-American Statue in Art and History*, catalog for a traveling exhibition of the New York Public Library and the Comité officiel Franco-Américain pour la celebration centenaire de la Statue de la Liberté (New York: Harper and Row, 1986).

13. Cf. June Hargrove, "The Power of the Press," in *Liberty*.

14. Some French recipients of Marshall Plan benefits wished we had made the gift with a confession that it also served American self-interest; such an acknowledgment would have reduced their sense of indebtedness to the United States. What we implied as our hope for "repayment" was anti-Communist votes, permission to station troops, and gratitude. None of the above corresponded to what the French wanted from us:

recognition of their earlier contributions to us, especially the Battle of Yorktown and the Statue of Liberty; consultations about French achievements in research and development during wartime; and acceptance of French knowledge about how to deal with the Islamic world from which we were trying to remove the French. Cf. my *Gifts and Nations* and "Allah Loves Strong Men," *Columbia University Forum* (Winter 1961).

15. Quoted in *New York Times*, July 20, 1925.

16. Bartholdi's pride was understandable when he declared: "It is a comfort to know that this statue will exist 1,000 years from now long after our names will be forgotten" (quoted in caption at exhibition at base of Statue of Liberty).

17. Cf. *France and the United States*, trans. Derek Coltman (Chicago and London: University of Chicago Press, 1978).

18. Text provided by Franklin D. Roosevelt Library, National Archives and Records Administration, Hyde Park, N.Y.

19. Ibid.

20. Cf. *New York Times*, December 3, 1916.

INDEX

Aboriginal inhabitants, 42
Abstract phenomena, 29
Acculturation, 18
Africa, 8, 103, 105n.26, 109, 110
    the Congo, 30
    first atomic reactor, 77n.16
    French aid to, 67
    Ghana, 30
    Islamic, 38
    Morocco, 20, 35
    Nambila people, 47n.33
    scholarships, 111n.8
    Sierra Leone, 49-50n.38
    study in, 19-20, 28
    young nations, 49-50n.38
Age-grading, 49, 49-50n.38, 64
Algeria, 30, 37, 38, 60, 66-67n.25, 79, 80, 109, 111n.8
"Allah Loves Strong Men" (Dillon), 61n.12, 129n.14
Almsgiving, 112
Alphand, Hervé, 78n.17
Alsop, 78n.17
Alternatives to countergifts, 74-81
Ambivalence, 54, 62, 71
America (ship), 145
American Anthropological Association, 20
American Committee, Sons of the American Revolution, 148
American Episcopalians, 77n.16
American Revolution, 151
Amsterdam University, 22
Ancient man, 13, 70, 106
Anglo-American schools, 32, 32-33n.42

Antagonistic acculturation, 25, 25-26n.29, 26
Anthropology, 17, 18
    graduate study, 19
    operational methods of, 18
Anti-American sentiments of French, 25-26n.29, 26, 37, 38, 74-75, 79, 108
Anti-colonialism, 37
Appleton, Nathan, Jr., 121
Arab League nations, 44n.24
Arab-Israel rivalry, 118
Arabs, 96n.3
Aramco, 80
Archaic societies, 13, 30, 47n.32, 72
Arensberg, Conrad, 9, 17n.7, 26, 26-27n.30, 45n.27, 47n.32, 48n.34, 86-87n.33, 102-103n.20
    "Behavior and Organization: Industrial Studies," 84, 84n.27, 28
    "Plant Sociology: Real Discoveries and New Problems," 82, 82n.21, 83, 83n.24
    "Study of Complex Civilizations, The," 20
Argonauts of the Western Pacific (Malinowski), 15, 15n.3, 27, 28
Argyris, 83
Aristotle's *Physics,* 96n.3
Asian civilization, 19, 56n.7
peaceful periods in Asian history, 100n.17
Association exchange relationships, 57
At the Sources of American Productivity
    summary, 69-70

Chapple, Eliot, 46n.31, 48n.34, 77n.13, 82, 82n.21, 96-97n.5, 102-103n.20
Chermayoff and Geisman, 125
Childhood training, 17, 54-55n.4
Children's birthday parties, 40n.7
China, 56n.7, 56-57n.8, 96n.3, 100n.17
 aid from Soviet Union, 30, 101
Chinook Indians, 47
"Christian Faith and Technical Assistance" (Mead), 104, 104n.24
Christian theologians, 97n.7
Christianity, 42, 42n.14, 43
Christopher, John B., 58-59n.9
Chrysanthemum and the Sword (Benedict), 21
Circular process of obligations, 28
Circular reciprocity, 101, 104n.24
Civil Rights legislation, 110
Civil War (U.S.), 121
Clark, Pearl Franklin, 51n.41
Clearinghouse for Research in Human Organization, director of, 8
Cleveland, Grover, 114, 122, 126
Clough, Shephard, 9
Coleman, James, 6
Colombo Plan, 30, 101
Colonial relationships, 28, 105n.26, 109
Coltman, Derek, 129n.17
Columbia University, 7, 9
Columbia University Research on Contemporary Cultures, 21
Columbia University Teachers College, 8
 Social and Philosophical Foundations of Education Department, 19
Comité France Actuelle, 81
Common Market, 107
Communication, 86-87n.33
Communication in donor-receiver relationships, 82, 85, 93
Communication of Ideas, The (Bryson), 19
Communication theory, 17, 18
Communications, 22, 25, 27-28, 27-28n.32
Communications engineers, 27, 27-28n.32
Communism, 35, 37, 38, 46, 63, 67, 76, 84, 112, 113n.12, 128n.14
Communities processes, 25
Comparative method in sociology, 29, 30
Compensatory mechanisms, 71, 73-74n.7, 80, 93

Comte, Auguste, 31
Conceptual analysis, 31
Conceptual frameworks, 17
Concrete phenomena, 29-30, 33, 54, 85, 95, 98, 106, 107
Condorcet, Marquis de, 31
Conflict of interest, 123
Conflict and substitute objects, 78n.18
Congo, 30
Consultation, 86, 86-87n.33, 112-113
Coon, Carleton, 46n.31, 77n.13, 96-97n.5
Cornwallis's surrender, 118
Coser, Lewis, 18n.10, 78n.18
Cosmological knowledge, 50, 50-51n.39
Countergifts, 72, 73n.5, 74-81, 82, 85, 86, 93, 95, 96n.3, 102, 113n.12
Cowan, Wayne H., 42n.16, 51n.43, 104n.24
Crespi, L., 23n.21
Criteria for the Life History (Dollard), 17, 17n.8
Cross-cultural communications, 14, 17, 18, 24-25n.24, 56n.7, 95, 111
Cross-cultural comparisons, 21, 40n.7, 47n.32
Cultural contexts of gift exchange, 40n.7
Cultural mediators, 27
Cultural Patterns and Technical Change (Mead), 19, 19n.13
Cultural relations, 108
Cultural shock, 113
"Cultural Transformation in Ecological Perspective" (Mead), 69n.29
Cultural transmission, 19, 25
Culture
 and individual behavior, 54-55n.5
 and personality, 54-55n.5
Cunnison, Ian, 13n.1, 30n.35, 31, 128n.4
Currency, 45n.27, 47n.32
Cybernetics, 27-28n.32
Czechoslovakia, 105n.26

Dances with Wolves (film), 115
Dargaud, Victor, *Statue de la Liberté de New York dans l'atelier du fondeur Bayet, rue de Chazelles, La,* 114
Daughters of the American Revolution, 120
Davis, Kingsley, 41n.11, 49-50n.38
De Gaulle, Charles, 5, 7, 34, 37, 38, 57, 63, 74-75n.9, 75, 75n.11, 80n.20, 83, 83n.23, 84, 107, 107n.1, 108, 109, 111, 113, 113n.123, 120, 124, 128n.9

European Defense Community pact, 37
European military defenses, 34
"European Recovery and American Aid"
    (committee report), 34
European recovery program, 7
European social science studies, 8
European study in U.S. factories, 35-36,
    56n.7, 64-68
Evans-Pritchard, E. E., 30, 31, 32-33n.42
Evarts, William, 121
Exchange institutions, 39
Exchange relationships of Monsieur B.,
    56, 57
Exchange in social relations, 6, 9, 13
    and mutual aid, 18
    systems for, 15
    see also Kula ring international
        ceremonial exchange
Exhibitionism-spectatorship, 40n.7
Expectation to return gifts, 45-46

Factual analysis, 31
Family exchange relationships, 57, 58-
    61
Family relationships, 56-57n.8
Faulkner, William, 92n.48
Faure, François-Félix, 37
Feedback, 27, 27-28n.32
Females, 115
Feminist movement, 115
Figaro, Le, 79
Firth, 32-33n.42
Fiske, Marjorie, 24n.23
FitzGerald, William H. G., 121
Fleischman, John, 127n.1
Forbes, R. J., 22, 22n.18
Ford Foundation, 8
Foreign aid, 13, 16, 42n.14, 93, 97, 108
    bilateral or multi-national, 101
    from France, 109
    and great power status, 48
    self-aspects of, 34, 45-46n.28
    Soviet Union and U.S., 38, 44
Foreign Gifts and Decorations Act
    (1966), United States Congress, 110
Foreign policy, 5, 76
Forest of Symbols (Turner), 115, 127n.2
Forgiving debts, 97
Fortune, Reo F., Sorcerers of Dobu, 91,
    91n.46
Foundation giving, 28
Fourastié, Jean, 68n.27
France, 92n.48

atomic bomb, 37, 38
bourgeois families in, 58-59n.9,
    80
contributions of, 62, 63n.17, 75,
    81
culture of, 18, 24, 24-25n.24
Economic Cooperation Agreement
    with U.S., 43n.18
economic statistics, 66-67n.25
economy of, 66-67n.25
educational reform, 37
Enlightenment period in, 141
gift obligations and practices in,
    58-62
'humiliation of gifts' from U.S.,
    27, 77, 85, 96
and independence, 34
living standards in, 36
receiver-pupil role, 35, 73
reciprocity with U.S., 118
Rodin sculpture, 111n.8
scientific research in synthetics, 36,
    66
Statue of Liberty gift, 114-129
technical assistance, 13
triangular relationships with Great
    Britain and U.S., 117-122
United States aid to, 55-56n.6
weakness from war, destruction,
    and death, 35, 37, 63
yearly round of give and take, 58-
    62
France Means Business (pamphlet), 81
Frank Leslie's Illustrated Newspaper, 122
Franklin, Benjamin, 119
Franklin D. Roosevelt Library, 129n.18
Free exchange, 90n.43
Free gifts, 72n.4, 97n.7, 106
French anthropology, 115
French Association for the Increase of
    Productivity (A.F.A.P.), 8, 69
"French Higher Education and the New
    Managerial Elite" (Dillon), 84n.26
French National Museum of Franco-
    American Friendship, 124-125
French quest for autonomy and reciproc-
    ity: summary and interpretations, 16,
    33, 34-38, 74
French Revolution, 124
French-speaking Canadians, 107
French-style (Cartesian) analysis of U.S.
    economy, 36
Freud, Sigmund, 75n.10

135

Functional reciprocity and human organization, 100-106
Furniss, Edgar J., 83n.22

Galbraith, John K., 48n.35
Gangs in Chicago, 85n.29
Generosity, rules of, 41, 43
Geneva summit conference (1955), 37
Geopolitical concerns, 41n.10
Geopolitical macrocosm, 33, 35-38, 74
German occupation of France, 5
Germany, 92n.48, 100n.18
    in Atlantic-nation pact, 35
Gernet, Jacques, 100n.17
Gestalt psychology, 69n.29
Ghana, 30, 103, 105n.26
    Nkrumah, President of Ghana, 109
G.I. Bill, 7
Gift behavior patterns, 103-104
Gift giving, 5, 18, 28
    bilateral giving, 52, 52n.44
    cultural contexts of, 40n.7
    downward giving, 49, 51, 54
    initiation of, 47-48, 48n.34
    in the late 1960s, 112
    and market transactions, 47, 47n.32
    self-interest aspects of, 34
    suspicion of, 123
    as total phenomena, 45
    universality of, 41n.10
    value of gifts, 45n.27
    valued by both parties, 115
Gift obligations and practices in France, 58-62
Gift, The: Forms and Functions of Exchange in Archaic Societies (Mauss), 13, 94n.1, 108n.3, 117, 128n.4,11
Gift-avoidance, 53
Gift-rejection, 53
Gift-returning mechanism, 87-93
Gifts and Nations: The Obligation to Give, Receive, and Repay (Dillon), 128n.5, 129n.14
Gimwali (trade), 89, 92
Giving. *See* Obligation to give
God-man relationships, 97
Goguel, Anne-Marie, 8
Gold crisis (1968), 109n.6
Gorer, Geoffrey, 24
Gouldner, Alvin, 73-74n.7
    "Reciprocity and Autonomy in Functional Theory," 33

Governor's Island, 117
Grant Foundation, 8
Grasse, 124
Gratitude and ingratitude, 112, 123
Great Britain
    Suez crisis, 37
    triangular relationships with France and U.S., 117-122
    U.S. independence from, 118
Great power status of United States, 48, 48n.35
Greece, 114
Greek thought, 96n.3
Gregariousness or sociability, 41n.11
Gross, L., 33n.43, 73-74n.7
Guetzkow, 83
Guinea, 103, 105n.26
Guizot, François, 128n.10
Gurvitch, G., 32

Haida tribal practices, 44, 48
Hailsham, Lord, 121
Halbwachs, Maurice, 31
Hall, Edward T., 86n.32
Hare, P., 101n.19
Hargrove, June, 128n.13
Harriman, William Averell, 34
Hartman, Arthur, 120
Harvard Business School, 64
Harvard University, 6, 7, 27, 34, 111n.8
Harwood Manufacturing Company, 82, 84-85
Hawthorne Plant, 82
Hazen Foundation, 8
Head of state, 41n.10
Heathens, 42
Heizer, Robert F., 47n.33
Held, 32-33n.42
Helen (in Trojan horse story), 114
Hellenism, 96n.3
Heller, Clements, 8-9
Henry V (Shakespeare), 118
Herrenschmidt, Jean-Roger, 8, 27
    Problems of Technical Assistance, 27, 55-56n.6
Herskovits, Melville, 32-33n.42, 72, 72n.3, 87n.34
Hierarchies in gift giving, 46-50, 50-51
High and low status, 40n.7, 46-50
Hinduism, 41
Hiroshima, 77n.16
Hisarlik, Turkey, 127n.1
Hispanic civilization, 112

Historical perspective, 94n.1, 96n.3
History of Ethnological Theory (Lowie), 32
Hitler, Adolph, 126
Hobart and William Smith College, 25
Hodsoll, Francis, 121
Holy places, 113
Homans, George, 6, 33, 48n.34, 82, 82n.21, 85n.29
Homeostasis, 32-33n.42
Hopi culture, 29
"How-to-do-it-ism," 68
Howe, Russell Warren, 109n.7
Hubert, 32
Human condition, 97, 98
Human groups, 41
Human organization
    and functional reciprocity, 100-106
    and public policy, 94, 99-106
Human relations (management practices), 36
Human social behavior, 6
Humanistic responsibility, 22
Humanists, 17
Humiliation of gifts from U.S. to France, 27, 77, 85, 96
Humphrey, Hubert, 110
Hunt, Morton M., 94n.1
Hunt, Richard H., 122, 128n.12
Hypotheses, 96, 96-97n.5

Iasigi, Joseph, 121
IBM, 107
Ibn Saud, 80
Ignorance, 52n.44
Immigrants, 140, 141
Impact (journal), UNESCO, 19, 22, 22n.18
In vivo inclusiveness, 17, 23
International Cooperation Administration, 106n.27
Incest rules and kinship structures, 31
Independence Day (July 4, 1986), 117
Independence Hall, 127n.3
India, 20, 20n.15, 30, 56n.7, 80, 95
Individual behavior and culture, 54-55n.5
Indo-China conflict, 26, 33, 35, 36, 37
Indochina, 109
Inductive methods, 18, 31, 68
Industrial Revolution, 151
Industrial societies, 42, 49, 70, 85-86n.30, 95, 106, 112, 113

Industrial sociology, 26, 28n.33, 81-86
Industrialization, 20
    in France, 9
Information theory, 17
Initiation of gift giving, 47-48, 48n.34
Institute of Ethnology, Musee de l'Homme (Paris), 19
Institute for Intercultural Studies in New York, 19
Institute of Religious and Social Studies, 98, 98n.9
Institutionalized reciprocity, 28, 71, 81, 95, 100n.17
Instruction versus information, 65-66, 65n.20
Intangible gifts, 39, 44, 51, 92
Intellectual debt, 7
Intellectual goods, 14
Intellectual differences, 67-68
Interaction, 17, 18, 25
Interchange in social relations, 6
Interdependence, 104
International ceremonial exchange of the *kula* ring. *See Kula* ring international ceremonial exchange
International Cooperation Administration, 111n.8
International philanthropy, 7
International relations, 6, 8, 94n.1, 100n.18
    reciprocity in, 18, 21-22n.17
International technical assistance. *See* Technical assistance
Interviews, 17, 18, 22n.19, 33
    with Monsieur B., 74-75n.9
    reciprocity and gift exchange in, 62-63n.16
Intra-cultural exchanges, 40, 40n.7
Introduction, 13-38
    French quest for autonomy and reciprocity: summary and interpretations, 16, 33, 34-38
    materials and methods: a natural history, 16-29
        first stage (1950-1952), 18-21
        second staqge (1952-1956), 21-24
        third stage (1956-1960), 25-29
    purposes, 13-16
    significance of Marcel Mauss, 16, 29-33
Irish, 73n.5

Isere (French ship), 115
Islam, 41, 76, 157n.14
"Islam and Authority Patterns in a French Factory: The Role of Kinship and Religion in Boss-Worker Relationships" (Dillon), 61n.12
Islamic Africa, 38
Israel, 44n.24
    aid to Ghana, 30, 105n.26
    Suez crisis, 37-37, 78, 79
Italy, 111n.8

James, William, 73-74n.7
Japan, 19, 21, 54-55n.4, 73n.5, 77, 92n.48, 96n.3, 98n.8, 100n.17, 111n.8
    aid to Algeria and India, 30
    cyclotron at Tokyo University, 77-78, 77n.16
Jay, John, 121
Jeanne d'Arc, 115
Jefferson, Thomas, 119, 127
Jewish Theological Seminary of America, New York City, 98n.9
Jews, East European, 49, 49n.37
Joffe, Natalie, 49, 49n.37
Jones, John Paul, 119, 124
Judaeo-Christian traditions, 41, 42, 42n.14
Jusserand, Jules J., 127
Justice, 112

Kaja, 69n.29
Kam, Henry, 108n.4
Kashmir, 80
Kazam and Monsieur B., 60-61
Kendall, Patricia, 24n.23
Kennedy Center for the Performing Arts, 111n.8
Kennedy Library, 111n.8
Kenny, Michael, 112
Keynsian theory, 45n.27
Khrushchev, Nikita, 37, 83, 83n.23, 84
Kimball, Solon T., 9, 17n.9, 86-87n.33
Kita-Kamakura, 98n.8
Kluckhohn, 32-33n.42
Knowledge as gift, 50-52
Knowledge and intellectual goods, 14, 71, 86, 95, 96, 105
Komarovsky, Mirra, 82n.21, 82n.24
Korean War, 35, 37
Kroeber, Alfred, 19, 50-51n.39, 67n.26, 75n.11, 82n.21, 83n.22, 108n.2
Krumm, John N., 98n.8

Kula ring international ceremonial exchange, 15, 28, 30, 40n.6, 41n.10, 81, 87-93, 95, 101-104, 104n.24, 105
Kwakiutl Indians, 27, 47n.33, 48, 49, 53, 73n.6, 95

Lafayette, Marquis de, 119, 121, 124
Lafayette-Rochambeau Society, 121
Landes, David S., 9
Language tutor for Monsieur B., 21-24
Larrabee, Eric, 42, 43n.17,18, 45n.28
Laswell, Harold, 23, 26, 27, 104n.22
Leadership in donor-receiver relationships, 83
Leadership as a form of inviting gifts, 100, 113
Lee, Muna, 75-76n.12
Leenard, Henry L., 75n.10
Legislators, 110
Lerner, Daniel, 21-22n.17, 23n.20, 25n.24
Lerner, Max, 48n.35
Levatard (Argentine frigate), 143
Lévi-Strauss, Claude, 6, 13n.1,2, 25n.27, 27-28n.32, 29, 31, 33, 83n.22, 99n.15, 128n.5
    Sociologie et Anthropologie, 32-33n.42, 33n.45, 95n.1, 128n.4
Lewin, Kurt, 25n.28, 80n.20, 83, 84, 84n.25
L'Express, 107
Leyden, 8
Liberty Bell, 127n.3
Liberty Day, 115
Liberty Enlightening the World (Bartholdi), 116, 121, 122, 125, 128n.12, 129n.16
    see also Statue of Liberty
Liberty Island, 125
Liska, Geeorge, 104, 104n.22
Loeb, E., 25n.29
Louis XIV (king of France), 119
Louis XV (king of France), 119
Louis XVI (king of France), 119
Louisiades, 87n.35
Louisiana Purchase, 119, 124
Lowie, Robert, 46n.31, 77n.13, 100n.18
    History of Ethnological Theory, 32
Luke, Steven, 108n.3

MacAloon, John, 127n.2
MacMillan, Harold, 83
Macrocosm, 33, 35-38, 74

Madame B., 8
Majority, 110
Malatesta, 107
Male and Female (Mead), 54-55n.5
Mali, 103
Malinowski, Bronislaw, 32-33n.42,
72n.4, 89-90n.42, 91n.46
Argonauts of the Western Pacific,
15, 15n.3, 27, 28, 30, 33, 87-
93
Management practices, 36
Managerial knowledge, 34
Mandarin scholars, 8
Mandelbaum, David G., 20, 20n.15,
56n.7
Maneul d'ethnographie (Mauss), 107
Manufacturing process, 34
Maori, 73n.5
Market transactions and gift giving, 47,
47n.32
Markets, 45n.27
Marsh, John O., Jr., 120
Marshall, George C., 7, 34
Marshall Plan, 5, 7, 21, 23, 24, 26, 34,
44, 46, 100n.18, 120, 124
anti-gratitude, 74n.8
cultural mediators, 27
downward giving, 49
French-American relations, 29, 40,
43, 63, 66-67n.25, 67, 74
and *kula* ring, 89-90n.42, 90, 92
and Mauss, 30
national self-interest, 43n.18
and potlatch ceremonies, 15
self-interest, 128n.14
as a system of gift exchange, 54-
55n.5
unfree nature of, 64
Marx, Karl, 33
Marxist theory, 45n.27
Masonic symbols, 125
Mass media, 19, 83n.23
Mass production, 36
Massignon, Louis, 20
Massim area of the Pacific, 87-93
Material culture, 50-51n.39
Materials and methods: a natural history.
See Introduction
Maulnier, Thierry, 79, 81
Mauss, Marcel, 6, 7, 8, 9, 12, 14, 15, 18,
26, 27, 106
death of, 31
and essays, 32

*Gift, The: Forms and Functions
of Exchange in Archaic Societies*, 13, 30, 31, 94n.1, 108n.3,
117, 128n.4,11
incest rules and kinship structures,
31
"Les techniques du corps," 32-
33n.42
Maneul d'ethnographie, 107
obligation theory, 28
on reciprocity, 27, 31, 33
significance of, 16, 29-33
Sociologie et Anthropologie, 25,
25n.26,27, 33, 33n.45
technical assistance, 13n.2
in "The Ultimate Gift," 117-118,
121, 128n.4,5
see also Obligations
Mayflower, 127n.3
Mayo, E., 82, 82n.21
McKnight, Robert K., 54-55n.4
McMurry, Ruth, 75-76n.12
Mead, George H., 54-55n.4
Mead, Margaret, 9, 16n.6, 19, 20n.16,
21, 32-33n.42, 51, 51n.43, 56-57n.8,
74n.9, 75n.11
"Christian Faith and Technical As-
sistance," 104, 104n.24
*Cultural Patterns and Technical
Change*, 19, 19n.13, 20n.14
"Cultural Transformation in Eco-
logical Perspective," 69n.29
Male and Female, 54-55n.5
religion and gifts, 42
*Study of Culture at a Distance,
The*, 40n.7, 49n.37
Themes in French Culture, 24
Medieval socialism, 112
Meknes, Morocco, 20
Melanesians, 15, 15n.3, 30, 39, 70,
73n.5, 87-93, 91n.46
Mendel, Gregor, 6
Menninger Foundation, 25
Merchants, 47n.32
Merton, Robert K., 24n.23, 82, 82n.21,
94n.1
Métraux, Alfred, 20
Métraux, Rhoda, 9, 20n.16, 24, 40n.7,
49n.37, 54-55n.4, 56-57n.8, 74n.9,
105n.25
Microcosm, 33, 35-38, 74
Middle East, 118
Military aid, 5

140

Prestige, 72n.4, 73
Prestige and peace as motive to give, 43-45, 48
Price, Harry Bayard, 55-56n.6
Primitive people. *See* Pre-literate people
Primitive religions, 41
Problems of Technical Assistance (Herrenschmidt), 27
Productivity, 14, 38, 68-71, 96n.3
Productivity practices in U.S., 36
Productivity teams, 34
Projective technique, 22, 22n.19
Property value, 45n.27
Prophets, 113
Protector-benefactor-teacher nation, 34, 35
Protestant ethic, 42
Pseudo reciprocity, 102-103
Psychai, 29, 30n.35
Psychiatry, 17
Psychoanalytic theories, 75n.10, 78n.18
Psychological alternatives to countergifts, 74-81
Psychology, 17
Psychosomatic medicine, 32-33n.42
Ptolemy's astronomy, 96n.3
Public policy, 18, 94, 99-106
Public servants, 110
Public service, 48n.35
Pulitzer, Joseph, 122-123
Punjab Village in Pakistan, A (Eglar), 40n.7
Pupil-receiver nations, 14, 51, 63, 86, 112
Purchasing power, 110
Pure gifts, 72n.4, 106
Pure reciprocity, 101-103
Purposes of study, 13-16
Pyle, John, 98n.8
Pyramidal pattern of gift behavior, 103n.21

Quebec, 108-109

Racism, white, 110
Radcliff-Brown, 32-33n.42
Ranger (ship), 119
Ranks of donors and recipients, 46-50, 50-51
Reagan, Ronald, 117
Receive, obligation to. *See* Obligation to receive
Receiver-pupil role of France, 35

Reciprocity
   between France and the United States, 118
   circular, 101, 104n.24
   functional reciprocity and human organization, 100-106
   for gift giving, 5, 9, 15, 54-55n.5
   institutionalized, 28, 71, 81
   and marriage, 85-86n.30
   in peer relationships, 86-87n.33
   styles of, 18
   two-way communication, 85, 85n.29
   in wars, 111
   see also Mauss, Marcel
"Reciprocity and Autonomy in Functional Theory" (Gouldner), 33
Red shell necklaces (soulava), 88, 91
Redfield, Robert, 32-33n.42, 54-55n.5
Reducing the weight of the obligation, 62-70
Rehfisch, Farnham, 47n.33
Religion, 97
Religion and Civilization Series, 98n.9
Religious exchange relationships, 57, 58, 59
Religious obligation in motives to give, 41-43
Renaissance Italy, 8
Renoir, Pierre-Auguste, 139
Repay, obligation to. *See* Obligation to repay
Research on human organization and public policy, 94, 99-106
Research methods, 96, 96-97n.5
Research propositions, 112-113
Reston, James, 78n.17
Revolution, 113n.12
Rice, Howard C., Jr., 128n.6
Richter, Mischa, 116
Riffian family organization, 46n.31
Ripley, S. Dillon, 120-121
Rite of passage (1986), 117
Rites de passage, 58, 59
Rochambeau's armies, 118, 124, 128n.6
Rockefeller Foundation, 111n.8
Rohrer, John H., 26-27n.30, 84n.28
Role differentiation, 100
Roman warriors, 116
Rome, 56n.7
Roosevelt, Franklin D., 37, 126, 129n.18
Roosevelt Library (Franklin D.), 129n.18
Rossel island, 87n.35

Rousseau, Jean-Jacques, 119
Rubber industry, 35
Rumania, 108
Rusk, Dean, 111, 111n.8
Russian emperors, 116

Sacred knowledge, 50, 50-51n.39
Safety-value mechanism, 87-93, 96n.4, 102
Sahlins, Marshall D., 113n.11
St. John the Divine Cathedral, 98n.8
St. Paul's Chapel, Columbia University, 98n.8
St. Paul's University, Tokyo, 77n.16
St. Simon, 31
Samoa, 73n.5
Sartin, Robert, Madame, 9
Scandinavian epic, the *Edda*, 99
Schalochmones (sweetmeats), 49n.37
Schematic summary. *See* French quest for autonomy and reciprocity: summary and interpretations
Schumpeter, Joseph, 104n.22
Secularization of puritan values, 42
Self-consciousness, 17
Self-esteem, 17, 102, 113
Self-interest motives, 41, 43, 43n.18, 44n.52, 72n.4, 110, 112, 114, 128n.14
Seligman, C. G., 87n.35
Serfs, 42
Servan-Schreiber, Jean-Jacque, *Le Défi Américain, Le,* 107
Seth, Ronald, 77n.13
Shakespeare, William, 78n.18
    Henry V, 118
Shapiro, L. J., 22n.19
Shared symbols, 41n.10
Shartle, 83
Sherif, M., 26-27n.30, 84n.28
Shifting symbolism, 116-117
Shintoism, 42n.14
Short-term versus long-term, 128n.8
Shub, Anatole, 108n.4
Sibling equivalences, 46n.31
Siegel, Bernard J., 25n.28
Sierra Leone, 49-50n.38
Sills, David L., 108n.3, 111n.10
Simmel, Georg, 78n.18
Simon, 83
Simpson, G., 90n.43
Slaves, 42, 49-50n.38
Small Groups, 101, 101n.19
Smithsonian Institution, 120, 121

Social arrangement around gifts, 46-50
Social change, 19
Social class conflict, 36
Social conflict, 18n.10, 110
Social isolation, 41n.11
Social and Philosophical Foundations of Education Department, Columbia University Teachers College, 19
Social relations, 6
Social sanctions, 41
Social science research center, 8
Social science studies
    in Europe, 8
    in the United States, 8
Social structures, 40n.7
Sociaux totaux (social whole), 32, 33, 54, 93, 95, 106, 107
Society for Applied Anthropology, 7-8
Society of Jesus, 77n.16
Sociologie et Anthropologie (Mauss), 25, 25n.26,27, 33, 33n.45
    introduction by Lévi-Strauss, 32-33n.42
Sociology, 17
Solomon Island, 85n.30
Sons of the American Revolution, American Committee, 122
Sorcerers of Dobu (Fortune), 91, 91n.46
Soulava (red shell necklaces), 88
South Asians, aid to, 44n.24
South Sea exchanges, 15
South Sea trade routes, 87n.35
South Vietnamese, 111
Soviet Union, 83-84, 105n.26, 109, 112
    aid to China and East European nations, 30, 101
    and De Gaulle, 128n.9
    prestige ratings, 44n.19
    Sputnik, 85-86n.30
    Tass (Soviet news agency), 107
    and U.S., 38, 44, 48
Sparta, 114
Specialization of industries, 92, 100
Spencer, Herbert, 90n.43
Spindler, C., 25n.28
Spiritual matter, 39
Spiritual values, 22
Standard Oil Company of New Jersey, 98, 98n.9
Starvation, 52n.44
Statue of Liberty, 62, 114-129
    domestication of, 127n.3
    electrification of, 128n.3

anti-colonialism, 37
as benefactor-teacher nation, 34
Cartesian analysis of U.S.
  economy, 36
contributions of France to, 62,
  63n.17
dollar, 109n.6
domestic problems, 110
donor-teacher role, 35, 49, 51, 63
Economic Cooperation Agreement
  with France, 43n.18
European study in factories, 35-
  36, 56n.7, 64-68
government of, 7, 51
great power status, 48, 48n.35
independence from Great Britain,
  118
industrial practices, 21
instruction versus information, 65-
  66, 65n.20
Judaeo-Christian traditions, 42
National Advisory Commission on
  Civil Disorders, 110
obligations to Europe, 34
Point Four program, 51, 53n.4
presidential campaign (1960), 43-44
prestige ratings, 44n.19
productivity teams, 34
as protector-benefactor-teacher
  nation, 34, 35
reciprocity with France, 117-118
social science studies in, 8
and Soviet Union, 38, 44, 48
Statue of Liberty gift from France,
  114-129
technical assistance, 13
triangular relationships with Great
  Britain and France, 117-122
youth culture, 66, 66n.23
United States Congress
  Eightieth Congress appropriation
    for Marshall Plan, 34
  Foreign Gifts and Decorations Act
    (1966), 110
United States State Department, 110
University of Nalanda, India, 56n.7
Universality of gifts, 41n.10, 70, 89-
  90n.42, 94
University of California at Berkeley, 18
University of Lovanium in the Congo,
  77n.16

University of Michigan, 100n.17
U.S.S.R. *See* Soviet Union

Value of gifts, 45n.27
Van Fleet, James, 78n.17
Vartan bhanji mechanism of gift ex-
  change, 40n.7
Vietcong, 111
Vietnam, 37, 109, 111, 111n.8
Vincent (Lorraine village), 61-62
Virgin Mary, 115

Wardle, H. N., 44-45, 45n.25, 73n.5
Warner, Lloyd, 32-33n.42
Wars, 53, 74, 99, 101
  reciprocity in, 111
Warsaw Pact, 108
Washington, George, 118, 119, 121, 124
Washington Monument, 122, 127-
  128n.3
Watson, G., 54-55n.4, 80n.20, 106n.27
Wax, Murray, 22n.19
Wax, Rosalie Hankey, 18n.11, 62-63n.16
Wayland, Sloan, 9
Weakland, John H., 9, 56-57n.8
Weber, Max, 8
Weiner, Norbert, 27-28n.32
Welfare, 110
West Alaskan Eskimo societies, 41
Western industrial civilization, 13, 19
Weston, Theodore, 121
White racism, 110
White-shelled bracelets (swali), 88, 91
Whitehead, Alfred North, 50-51n.39
Whole, social, 32, 33, 54, 93, 95, 106, 107
Whyte, William F., 48n.34, 82, 82n.21,
  85n.29
Wilson, Woodrow, 127-128n.3
Woodlark Island, 87n.35
World Book, 123
World equilibrium, 109n.6
World Federation of Mental Health, 19
World responsibility, 48, 48n.35

Yearly round of give and take in France,
  58-62
Yemen, 80
Yorktown, 118-122, 129n.14

Zen Buddhism, 98n.8
Znaniecki, Florian, 50-51n.39, 65n.21